OUTDOOR COOKING for KIDS

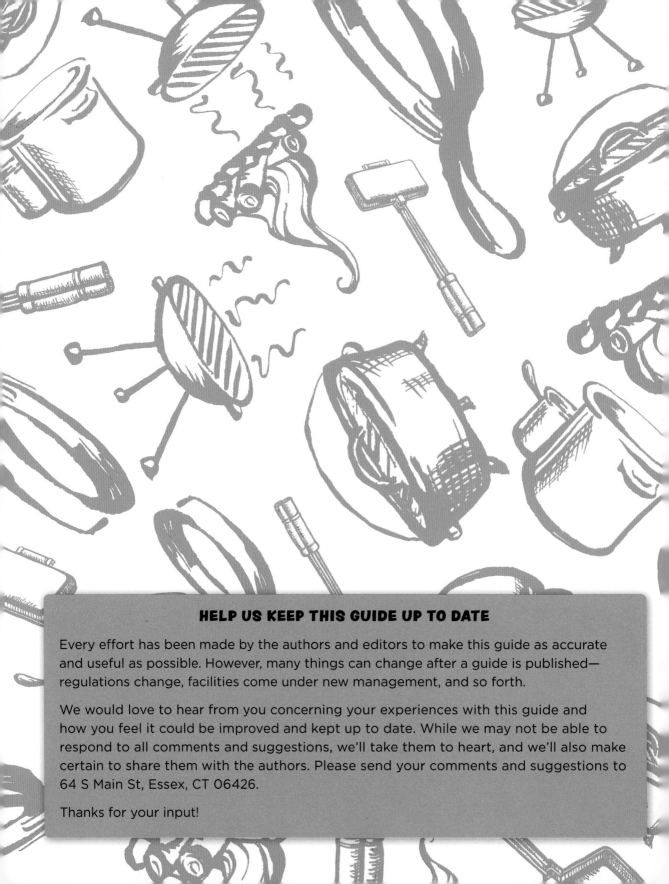

HELP US KEEP THIS GUIDE UP TO DATE

Every effort has been made by the authors and editors to make this guide as accurate and useful as possible. However, many things can change after a guide is published—regulations change, facilities come under new management, and so forth.

We would love to hear from you concerning your experiences with this guide and how you feel it could be improved and kept up to date. While we may not be able to respond to all comments and suggestions, we'll take them to heart, and we'll also make certain to share them with the authors. Please send your comments and suggestions to 64 S Main St, Essex, CT 06426.

Thanks for your input!

OUTDOOR COOKING for KIDS

The Essential Culinary Guide to Increasing Confidence, Safety, and Enjoyment in the Wild

BUCK TILTON • CHRISTINE CONNERS

FALCON®

Essex, Connecticut

An imprint of The Globe Pequot Publishing Group, Inc.
64 South Main Street
Essex, CT 06426
www.globepequot.com

Falcon and FalconGuides are registered trademarks, and Make Adventure Your Story is a trademark of Globe Pequot Publishing Group, Inc.

Distributed by NATIONAL BOOK NETWORK

Illustrations by Christine Conners

Photos by Buck Tilton and Christine Conners unless noted otherwise

British Library Cataloguing in Publication Information available

Library of Congress Cataloging-in-Publication Data

Names: Tilton, Buck, author. | Conners, Christine, author.
Title: Outdoor cooking for kids : the essential culinary guide to increasing confidence, safety, and enjoyment in the wild / Buck Tilton and Christine Conners.
Description: Essex, Connecticut : Falcon Guides, [2025] | Includes index. | Audience: Grades 4-6
Identifiers: LCCN 2024042470 (print) | LCCN 2024042471 (ebook) | ISBN 9781493084708 (paperback) | ISBN 9781493084715 (epub)
Subjects: LCSH: Outdoor cooking—Juvenile literature.
Classification: LCC TX823 .T55 2025 (print) | LCC TX823 (ebook) | DDC 641.5/78—dc23/eng/20241029
LC record available at https://lccn.loc.gov/2024042470
LC ebook record available at https://lccn.loc.gov/2024042471

Important: *Never,* ever use a heat source (campfire, stove) hot enough to cook food *without adult supervision.*

CONTENTS

INTRODUCTION

A very long time ago—nobody knows how long—there was no cooked food. When anyone ate anything, whatever got eaten was raw. There were choices, all cold and many tough to chew, such as leaves, berries, roots, flowers, un-grilled wooly mammoth. Another mystery is this: no one knows when cooking started. Maybe something got cooked first when a cave dweller

accidentally dropped a prehistoric rabbit foot into a fire. By the time they raked it out of the coals, it was, yep, cooked. And it tasted so much better! Cooking was here to stay.

When you cook something, as you know, you apply heat to the something until it becomes tastier (usually), easier to digest, often more nutritious, and safer (since cooking can kill germs). You also know there are lots of different ways to apply heat to food other than throwing it into a fire. To name some, there's boiling, frying, grilling, and baking. And those ways to cook can be done outdoors. Welcome to cooking outdoors!

CAMPFIRE BASICS

Great camping stoves are available for cooking outdoors. Some of the recipes in this book work well on a camping stove, especially the boiling recipes. But we decided to focus on cooking with a fire. It's more of a challenge, but it's a lot more fun. It's also more dangerous, and safety needs to be your first priority. Follow these safety guidelines:

1. Never start a fire without an adult present.
2. Always have a bucket of water and shovel nearby.
3. Avoid starting fires on windy days.
4. Never let a fire get too big or out of control.
5. Never play with fire.
6. Never play around a campfire.
7. Always put your fire out completely when you leave (there's more on this later).

THE UPS AND DOWNS OF COALS

Knobs on your stove at home let you increase the heat, under a pot or pan, or decrease the heat. That's great because some cooking works best at high heat, some at low heat, and some in between. There are no knobs on a campfire. But if you carefully scrape the coals together into a mound under your pot or pan with long-handled tongs, the heat increases. And if you spread the coals out, the heat under your pot or pan decreases. Who needs a knob?

To build a fire:

1. Build a fire only in spots designated as fire places. Most campgrounds have places for fires. Some of these fire places have built-in grills, and that's a big bonus. If there are no fire places, and if fires are allowed, build your fire on dry, non-vegetated soil (it's just dirt, nothing is growing there).

2. Gather a large pile of dry material—dead grass, old pine needles, paper-like bark—to use as tinder. Tinder is small stuff that burns easily.

3. Gather a lot of kindling: small, dry twigs. Kindling is bigger than tinder but still burns pretty quickly.

4. Gather several armloads of fuel: dry pieces of wood, wood that snaps when you break it.

5. Build a pyramid of tinder, fluffing it so air can circulate through.

6. Over the tinder build a loose pyramid of kindling.

7. When all is ready, set a flame to the tinder. When the kindling is fully involved, start adding progressively larger pieces of fuel, arranging things loosely to allow air to flow through. Add fuel slowly until the fire is the desired size, but keep it small. A small fire saves fuel and burns down to cooking coals faster than a big fire. And please remember that putting out fires you build is very important. When you walk away for the last time from a fire, be sure it is completely out.

Putting out a fire:

1. Let the fire burn down to ash naturally.
2. Pour lots of water over the campfire to drown the embers and stop the hissing sounds.
3. Use a shovel to stir and cover any remaining coals.
4. Make sure all the embers are buried and out. Add sand or dirt if necessary.

RUMENA

JOHNER IMAGES

Edible Campfire

This is fun practice in campfire building.

1 medium-size flour tortilla
1 tablespoon peanut butter
About 30 mini marshmallows or mini jelly beans
1 teaspoon sweetened coconut flakes
3 small pretzel sticks
1 large pretzel stick
5 Red Hots candies or candy corn

EQUIPMENT:

Paper plate
Small paper cup

PREPARATION:

1. Lay your tortilla flat on your paper plate.
2. Spread the peanut butter into a circle about the size of a baseball at the center of the tortilla. This will help keep the other pieces in place.
3. Surround the peanut butter with a circle of mini marshmallows or jelly beans. These are the "campfire stones" to make your "fire ring."
4. Pile some coconut flakes in the center of the ring. This is the "tinder."
5. Break small pretzel sticks in half and pile the pieces over the coconut flakes. This is the "kindling."
6. Break a large pretzel stick into three pieces, then lay the pieces on top of each other to form a triangle over the kindling. These are the "logs."
7. Lay the Red Hots candies or candy corn among the kindling to form the "fire."
8. Fill the paper cup with the water you should have nearby to put out a real fire, but since this isn't a real fire, drink it up!

Servings: 1 (multiply as required)
Preparation time: 15 minutes

Smokey Bear

If you've already done some camping, and even if you haven't, you probably know about Smokey Bear. Smokey remains a symbol and reminder of the need to exercise extreme caution anytime we use fire. A single careless act can destroy forests and homes, and sadly can take the lives of both humans and animals. But did you know Smokey was a real bear?

During the 1940s the United States Forest Service (USFS) launched a forest fire prevention campaign that featured posters of a cute bear cub named Smokey. Later, in 1950, a real bear cub was rescued from a tree during a forest fire in New Mexico. The rescued cub was originally named Hotfoot Teddy because his paws had been burned in the fire. His name was later changed to Smokey, to align with the forest fire prevention posters.

Smokey Bear quickly became a real-life celebrity and spent the rest of his life entertaining visitors at the National Zoo in Washington, DC. Over the years, Smokey's appearance has changed, but his message of forest fire prevention has stayed the same.

HOW DO CAMPFIRES START FOREST FIRES?

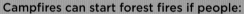

Campfires can start forest fires if people:

- let their fire get too large and out of control;
- leave their campfire unattended while it's still burning; or
- don't put their fire out completely.

Can You Read the Sign?

ASHLEY COOPER

TOBIAS TITZ

It's hard to imagine camping without a campfire, but when fire conditions are unsafe, it can happen. No campground is the same, so it's important to know the specific fire safety regulations for your area. Look for signs at the entrance to your park or speak to a forest ranger to understand the current conditions in your area.

Campgrounds have different rules about fire use, and these rules can change with the weather and seasons. Some campgrounds might provide ready-to-go fire rings complete with grills; other campgrounds forbid campfires altogether. Because it's possible that fires might be banned at your campground due to seasonal conditions, it's always good to have a backup cooking method ready!

AVID_CREATIVE

Don't Get Burned!

Even though you're going to be very careful, there's always a chance you might get burned. If you do, immediately soak the burned skin in cold water. It might be tender later, and a burn ointment or aloe might help. If you use an ointment, be sure it says "burn ointment" on the package. If blisters form, cover them with soft gauze or soft clothing and find a doctor.

DEEPBLUE4YOU

WATER AND FOOD SAFETY

Clean water is essential for drinking, and it's best for cooking. However, water can look clean and still make you really sick. Most campgrounds provide potable (safe to drink) water, but some don't. Many campers bring their own water, just in case. If your campground doesn't provide clean drinking water, and if you didn't bring enough, here are some things you can do:

SOLSTOCK

- **Boil it.** Water heated to the boiling point is free of disease-causing germs. A lengthy boil is not required.

YASSER CHALID

Boiling water is an effective way to kill germs.

- **Filter it.** Different outdoor water filters accomplish different things, so before you buy a water filter, read the directions carefully to learn exactly what it can and can't do.

- **Chemically disinfect it.** Iodine is often the preferred chemical to disinfect water at camp. Follow the directions on the label of any chemical you use.

CANVAN IMAGES

Water filters are one way to ensure your water is safe to drink.

Food poisoning happens when harmful germs in food get in you and make you sick. Here are some tips to help avoid food poisoning.

Food handling:
Before you start cooking, and after touching raw meats or eggs, wash your hands using soap and water. Dirty hands can spread harmful germs.

ANGELO DESANTIS

Food storage:
1. Always cover your food to protect it from floating microbes and disease-spreading insects like flies.
2. When you can, store foods at a close-to-freezing temperature to help prevent the growth of any germs that may already be on your food.
3. Keep foods and food containers properly sealed and on ice

JUANA MARI MOYA

in a cooler until it's time to prepare the meal. Place any leftovers in a sealed food-storage container on ice immediately following the meal.

Cross contamination:
When harmful germs move from one place to another, it's called cross contamination. Your food can get contaminated in ways you might not think about.

1. Mixing bowls, knives, and cutting boards can become con-

EDWIN TAN

taminated while working with raw meats and eggs. Keep contaminated utensils away from cooked foods or those that will be served raw, such as salads and fresh fruits and vegetables.

2. When storing food on ice, it's important to keep raw meat and eggs in their own separate cooler. As ice melts, the cold water can penetrate the items in the cooler. Whatever nasties may have been on the meat or eggs will find their way into the cold water.

3. For this reason, raw vegetables and fruits, condiments in containers, or leftovers should be kept in their own separate cooler away from the raw meat. Bottled or canned beverages, drinking water, and ice you'll put in a drink are best stored in a third cooler.

Cooking:

All foods containing raw meats or eggs must be thoroughly cooked to a temperature high enough to kill harmful microbes. The optimum cooking temperature depends on the type of food being cooked, but a good rule for all meats is to cook them to a temperature of at least 165°F. This will guarantee the elim-ination of all harmful food patho-

Steak and potatoes

gens. Use a food thermometer and carefully take multiple temperature mea-surements, especially in thicker areas of meat. If you have to guess when the meat is done, check to make sure all the pink is gone.

Blood-borne germs:

If a cook cuts themself while prepar-ing food, they should stop what they are doing to avoid contaminating the items they are preparing with blood. If blood comes in contact with the food, throw out the food. (Also, if you have a runny nose or are sick, you should leave the cooking to someone else.)

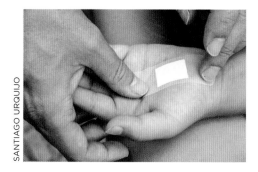
SANTIAGO URQUIJO

Cleaning your cookware:

1. Once you're done cooking, you'll need to clean your own dishes by hand. Before you start washing dishes, begin by washing your own hands first.
2. Scrape any remaining food on plates into the trash.
3. Fill one large plastic tub with hot soapy water (use biodegradable soap) for cleaning and another with only hot water for rinsing. You may need help making hot water if you are boiling it over a campfire. Add cooler water to the hot water as necessary so you don't get burned!
4. Scrub the cookware well using a natural sponge or scrubber if possible. Continue to use the soapy water to remove any remaining food. Once each item is cleaned, move it to the plain hot water tub for rinsing.
5. Once you're sure your cookware is clean, you can either air-dry it on a clean cloth (not directly on the picnic table) or hand-dry it. Store your clean cookware in a place that will remain clean for the next meal.
6. Water from the tubs should be disposed of in a manner that doesn't hurt the environment. Catch any remaining food particles from the tub using a strainer, and place the food particles with the rest of your trash so it doesn't attract animals. The remaining water can be poured into camp utility sinks, designated areas that accept gray or wastewater, or areas of natural vegetation. Never discard the water directly into a natural water source like a lake or river.

SCOTT SIMERLY

Poisonous plants:

The safest thing to do is *never* eat anything found in the wild unless you are totally sure it's safe to eat. But if you swallow something that might be poisonous, drink as much water as possible. Water dilutes the poison. Don't try to vomit. It's just not safe. If something poisonous was swallowed, the best action is to head for a doctor. Be prepared to tell the doctor what was eaten, when you ate it, and how much you ate.

If you get sick:

Signs of food poisoning can come within hours or even weeks after exposure. Common symptoms of food poisoning include:

- Diarrhea
- Upset stomach or nausea
- Vomiting
- Stomach cramps
- Fever
- Headaches

Sometimes food poisoning can lead to more-serious complications that require hospitalization. If your symptoms include dehydration, bloody diarrhea, or diarrhea for more than three days; fever of over 102°F; or excessive vomiting where you can't keep liquids down, you should see a doctor right away!

HIMARKLEY

OUTDOOR COOKING GEAR

If you want to be a good outdoor cook, you need to think about what you'll need when you get to camp. What you bring will depend on where you camp and the methods you plan to use to prepare your meals—and lots of info about different methods is in the next section of this book. While every trip is different, and many of your decisions will be based on what food you want to cook, we've put together a list of everything you might want. Sure, you won't need all this stuff, but you can pick from the list.

- Coolers, depending on the size of your group. Things you want to keep cool include meats and eggs, cheese, some veggies, beverages, and ice for cold drinks.
- Sturdy folding tables (if the campground doesn't have tables)
- Cooking pot (one that can go over very hot coals)
- Frying pan (one that can go over, yep, very hot coals)
- An assortment of measuring cups and spoons
- A couple knives, and sheaths or containers for the knives
- Cutting board
- Can opener (unless you have no cans to open)
- Bowls, an assortment of small, medium, and large sizes
- Long-handled wooden spoon
- Long-handled spatula (for flipping pancakes, eggs, etc.)
- Long-handled serving ladle
- Long-handled tongs
- Hand sanitizer
- Paper towels
- Cooking spray or vegetable oil, for greasing frying pans and Dutch ovens
- Heavy-duty aluminum foil
- Serving ware (dishes, bowls, plates, cups, etc.) for everybody
- Paper napkins
- Ziploc freezer bags, quart and gallon sizes
- Two washbasins for dirty dishes
- Pad to scrub the dirty dishes with
- Biodegradable dish detergent
- Heavy-duty trash bags
- Heavy gloves
- Long-neck lighter or two to start the fire
- Bins of appropriate size for storing kitchen gear

KNIFE SAFETY

A lot of the recipes in this book require food to be cut with a knife. And it's no surprise that cooks sometimes cut themselves. The injuries are usually not serious—but sometimes they are. It's important to follow some basic safety rules:

1. Never use a knife without permission from an adult.
2. Knives are not toys. Don't play with them.
3. Keep your knives away from the edge of the table, where they might fall on a foot.
4. Approach all knives as if they were sharp. Looks can be deceiving.
5. Always cut over a solid surface like a table. Don't cut on your lap or leg.

SCOTT SIMERLY

Can you spot a knife safety concern in this photo?

6. Be sure the handle of your knife is dry when in use. Wet knives can slip.
7. Place your knife back in its sheath (if it has one) after washing. If working with a pocketknife, be sure to close it after washing it. Put all knives away when not in use.
8. Keep knives away from your younger friends or siblings.
9. Make sure other campers are at least an arm's length away from you when you start cutting.
10. Avoid cutting something you're holding in your hand.

Knife techniques vary, but here's our personal favorite: With the knife facing away from you, and blade down, place your thumb on one side of the handle near the blade. Place your middle finger against the opposite side of the handle. Your thumb and middle finger should press against the handle to hold it still. Place your pointer finger firmly above the blade to help apply pressure from above. This technique will give you three points of control.

Look at the illustrations below: Do you recognize our suggested way of holding a knife? Can you tell which ones aren't good form? (See answers below.)

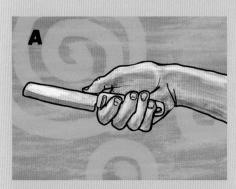

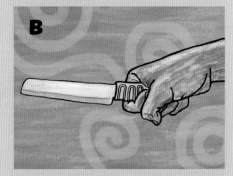

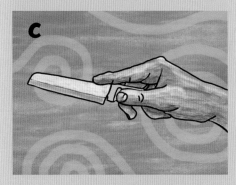

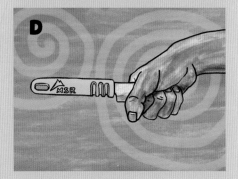

Answers:
A: Incorrect. B: Incorrect. C: Correct. D: Ouch! No! Incorrect!

What to Do If You Get Cut

Even when you know how to hold a knife correctly, cuts can happen. They're usually not very serious, but if you're bleeding, apply pressure with your clean hand directly to the cut and elevate the site higher than your heart. When the bleeding has stopped, do what you can to prevent infection. Clean the wound; irrigation works best. You can use a water bottle with a squirt top or punch a pinhole in a plastic bag. Irrigate with at least one quart of water.

After cleaning, if the width of the wound is less than a quarter-inch, pull the edges back to their original position with thin strips of tape. Cover the closed cut with antibiotic ointment, and apply a Band-Aid or sterile gauze with tape. If the width of the wound is a half inch or more, cover it with sterile gauze and tape and see a doctor.

KMATIJA

WESTEND61

Ways to Cook

Boiling

Bringing water to a boil and then putting something in the water until it cooks could be the easiest way to get food ready to eat. But you have to have a pot, or a pan, or a can—something to boil the water in. You can boil just about anything that fits into your pot (or pan, or can).

How much water you put in the pot depends on what you're cooking. Sometimes the amount of water doesn't matter much, like when you're boiling an egg or a carrot. Sometimes the amount of water matters a lot, like when you're making Porcupine Soup. We have included how much water to use in recipes that require boiling.

You can boil in a Dutch oven too!

How long you leave the food in the boiling water also depends on what you're cooking. Some foods are ready to eat after a couple of minutes. Some foods seem to take forever, especially when you're hungry. And, yes, we have included boiling times in the recipes.

You can use water from a lake or a stream, but remember you need to (1) pick out the sticks and leaves, and (2) bring the water to a boil before you put in any food so that any germs in the water are killed.

YELLOW DOG PRODUCTIONS

Note: You may know that water boils at 212°F—unless your outdoor adventure takes you high in the mountains. At higher elevations, water boils at lower temperatures. But all boiling water, no matter the elevation, has one thing in common: it's hot! So be careful.

Measuring Tools

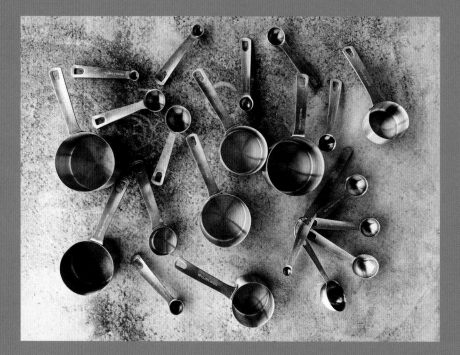

Ingredients are usually the first thing you see in a recipe. Sometimes an ingredient can be simple, like "1 banana." Other times you'll need to use measuring spoons or cups.

Teaspoons and tablespoons are used to measure smaller amounts of ingredients like spices. Measuring spoons come in the following sizes:

1 tablespoon	½ teaspoon
½ tablespoon	¼ teaspoon
1 teaspoon	⅛ teaspoon

Measuring cups are used to measure larger amounts of ingredients. They come in these sizes:

1 cup	½ cup
¾ cup	¼ cup
⅓ cup	

Measuring cups and spoons are interchangeable. For example, if a recipe calls for 1 cup of flour, you could use:

One 1 cup
Two ½ cups
Three ⅓ cups

Four ¼ cups
Or 16 tablespoons!!

Here's a handy conversion chart that will make things easier:

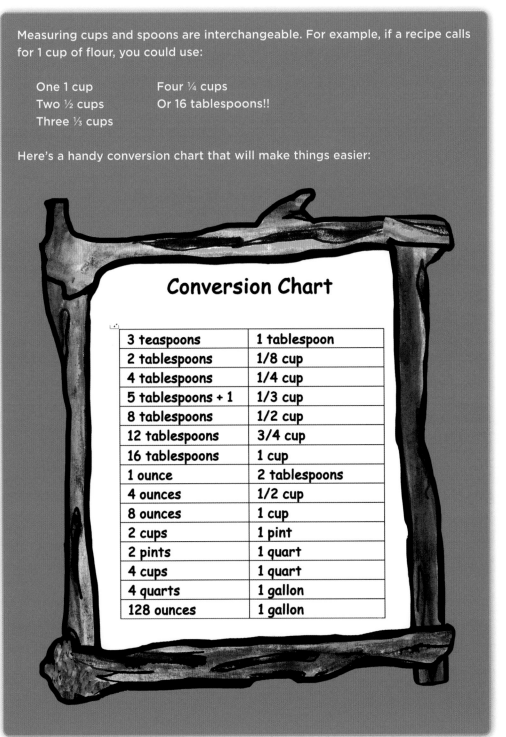

Conversion Chart

3 teaspoons	1 tablespoon
2 tablespoons	1/8 cup
4 tablespoons	1/4 cup
5 tablespoons + 1	1/3 cup
8 tablespoons	1/2 cup
12 tablespoons	3/4 cup
16 tablespoons	1 cup
1 ounce	2 tablespoons
4 ounces	1/2 cup
8 ounces	1 cup
2 cups	1 pint
2 pints	1 quart
4 cups	1 quart
4 quarts	1 gallon
128 ounces	1 gallon

BOILING RECIPES

Fabulous Fruit Oatmeal

2 cups whole milk

1 cup water

1 cup quick-cooking oatmeal

2 teaspoons brown sugar

½ cup dried fruit (your choice)

1 dash salt

⅓ cup cashew pieces

1 banana

EQUIPMENT:

Small cook pot

Long-handled spoon

PREPARATION:

1. Bring the milk and water to a boil in the cook pot.
2. Immediately add the oatmeal, brown sugar, dried fruit, and salt.
3. Reduce heat to a simmer and stir for 1 minute.
4. Add the cashews, stir, then remove from heat.
5. Top the oatmeal with sliced banana and serve.

Option: You can substitute regular oatmeal for the quick-cooking oatmeal, but simmer for about 5 minutes longer in step 3.

Servings: 4–6

Preparation time: 15 minutes

Porcupine Soup

The meatballs really look like small porcupines!

1 medium-size onion
1 pound lean ground beef
1 cup Minute Rice
¼ teaspoon salt
1 egg
2 (10.75-ounce) cans condensed
    tomato soup
2 (10.75-ounce) cans water (use
    empty soup can to measure)
Optional: shredded cheese, croutons

AZMANL

EQUIPMENT:

Medium-sized mixing bowl
Medium-sized cook pot
Knife

PREPARATION:

1. Chop up the onion.
2. Combine the onion, beef, rice, salt, and egg in a bowl.
3. Gently knead the meat mixture (yep, use your hands—after washing them) to combine the ingredients, then form small, bite-size balls.
4. In the cook pot, combine the tomato soup and water and bring to a boil.
5. Immediately reduce heat to a simmer, then put each beef ball on a large spoon and lower it gently into the soup.
6. Cover the pot and cook on low heat for about 30 minutes, until meatballs are fully cooked.
7. Add optional shredded cheese and/or croutons on top.

Servings: 6–8
Preparation time: 45 minutes

International Food Matchup!

You probably know that the United States is a melting pot of culinary delights. But do you know where these dishes were invented? The answers might surprise you!

Sushi _____

French fries _____

Cheesecake _____

Chicken tikka masala

_____

Chop suey _____

Fajitas _____

Hot dogs _____

Hot chocolate

_____

Sushi: When you think of sushi, you probably think of the modern version from Japan. But the original form of sushi, a type of preserved fish with fermented rice, is believed to have originated in China!

French fries: Don't let the name fool you. French fries are thought to have their roots in Belgium, where they were enjoyed with a variety of different condiments including mayonnaise!

Cheesecake: Believe it or not, cheesecake goes all the way back to the ancient Greeks. Had you attended the Olympic games in 776 BC, you could have enjoyed an ancient version of this dessert!

Chicken tikka masala: If you've visited an Indian restaurant you've probably seen this popular dish on the menu. But surprise! Tikka masala was invented by a chef from Bangladesh who was living in Scotland, so technically the dish comes from Scotland.

Chop suey: A staple in most Chinese restaurants, it's hard to believe that chop suey is thought to have originated in the United States! Truth is, there's a bit of a debate as to when and where the first chop suey recipe was created. Most agree it was invented by a Chinese chef, somewhere in the United States. Some think it may be a modification of a Cantonese dish called *tsap seui*, which means "miscellaneous leftovers."

Fajitas: Mexican restaurants serve up lots and lots of fajitas, a delicious dish of meat and vegetables served on a sizzling hot cast-iron skillet. The story of fajitas is actually "Tex-Mex." Fajitas began as an authentic cowboy recipe created by Mexican cattle ranchers working in Texas. But it wasn't until the early 1970s that this dish became popular in restaurants in southern Texas and later the world.

Hot dogs: Can there be a food more American than hot dogs? They're not as all-American as you might think. Today both Germany and Austria claim to be the originators of this popular snack.

Hot chocolate: Where did the first cup of hot chocolate come from? Well, you might be interested to know that the Mayans, from Central America and southeastern Mexico, were enjoying a version of this drink as early as 500 BC. Their "hot chocolate" had a kick, as it was a mix of ground cocoa seeds, cornmeal, and chili peppers. Oh, and it wasn't hot, it was served cold!

Dr Pepper Pork and Beans

1 small onion

1 tomato

1 bell pepper, any color

½ pound summer sausage

1 (28-ounce) can pork and beans

½ cup brown sugar

½ teaspoon ground cloves

1 (8-ounce) can crushed
   pineapple, drained

1 (12-ounce) can Dr Pepper
   (yes, the soda)

JULIEN MCROBERTS

EQUIPMENT:

Can opener

Medium-sized pot

Knife

PREPARATION:

1. Chop up the onion, tomato, bell pepper, and sausage, and combine with the remaining ingredients in a pot.
2. Bring to a boil, then immediately reduce heat to a simmer.
3. Continue to cook for about 30 minutes before serving.

Servings: 6–8
Preparation time: 45 minutes

Silly Cowboy Jargon

HILL STREET STUDIOS

When most people think about cowboys, they usually picture wide-brimmed hats, cattle drives, and rodeos. But did you know that cowboys had their own jargon (made-up words)? Cowboys did a lot of outdoor cooking, and so maybe it's not surprising that they spent their free time making up silly names for the things they ate.

Let's see if you can guess which cowboy name goes with the word we commonly use today. Write down the words you think match and check your answers below.

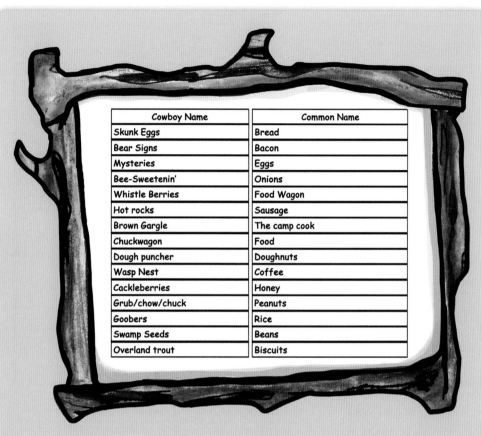

Cowboy Name	Common Name
Skunk Eggs	Bread
Bear Signs	Bacon
Mysteries	Eggs
Bee-Sweetenin'	Onions
Whistle Berries	Food Wagon
Hot rocks	Sausage
Brown Gargle	The camp cook
Chuckwagon	Food
Dough puncher	Doughnuts
Wasp Nest	Coffee
Cackleberries	Honey
Grub/chow/chuck	Peanuts
Goobers	Rice
Swamp Seeds	Beans
Overland trout	Biscuits

ANSWERS:

1. Skunk eggs: Onions
2. Bear signs: Doughnuts
3. Mysteries: Sausage
4. Bee-sweetenin': Honey
5. Whistle berries: Beans
6. Hot rocks: Biscuits
7. Brown gargle: Coffee
8. Chuckwagon: Food wagon
9. Dough puncher: The camp cook
10. Wasp nest: Bread
11. Cackleberries: Eggs
12. Grub/chow/chuck: Food
13. Goobers: Peanuts
14. Swamp seed: Rice
15. Overland trout: Bacon

Silly jargon fun: Make up a silly name for one of the foods you regularly eat and casually use your new word around your friends and family to see how they respond.

Quick Clam Chowder

2 (10-ounce) cans whole baby
    clams, undrained
4 green onions, chopped
1 (14.5-ounce) can diced new
    potatoes, drained
1 (15-ounce) can corn, drained
1 (15-ounce) can white
    beans, drained
2 tablespoons butter
1 (12-ounce) can evaporated milk
¼ teaspoon salt
Ground black pepper (amount
    depends on your taste buds)

EQUIPMENT:

Medium-sized pot
Can opener

PREPARATION:

1. Combine all of the ingredients in a pot.
2. Warm the chowder over medium heat for 10 to 15 minutes, then serve.

Servings: 4–6
Preparation time: 15 minutes

Octopus Ramen

This recipe is sure to get a few laughs. Once the hot dogs are sliced, they curl in the pot to look like octopuses!

8 hot dogs
6 green onions
4 (3-ounce) packets ramen
    noodles, your choice of flavor
6 cups water

EQUIPMENT:

Knife
Medium-sized cook pot
Wooden spoon

PREPARATION:

1. Using a knife, slice a hot dog lengthwise from one end to about halfway down along its length (and be careful). Don't cut it along the entire length, or it will fall apart.
2. The cut end of the hot dog now consists of two flaps. Use the knife to slit each flap down its length two or three more times to turn it into strips that are still joined to the uncut end of the hot dog. This bundle of strips will be the "tentacles," or arms of the octopus, while the uncut end of the hot dog will be the octopus's head.
3. Do this for each of the hot dogs, then place them in the cook pot.
4. Cut the ragged top parts from the green onions with a knife and throw them in the trash bag. Remove the stringy roots too. Chop the rest of the onions into small pieces and place them in the pot.
5. Add the noodles and flavoring mix from the packets of ramen noodles to the pot, then pour in the water.
6. Place the pot on the stove and set the flame to its highest setting. Bring the water to a boil while stirring occasionally with a wooden spoon.
7. Cook for 3 to 5 minutes until the noodles become soft and the "tentacles" of the hot dog octopuses begin to curl.
8. Serve carefully. The octopuses are hot!

Servings: 8
Preparation time: 30 minutes

Scrambled Chili Dogs

2 small onions

8 hot dogs

3 (15-ounce) cans chili

8 hot dog buns

1 (8-ounce) package shredded
   cheddar cheese

SERRNOVIK

EQUIPMENT:

Knife

Small bowl

Medium-sized cook pot

Can opener

Long-handled spoon

PREPARATION:

1. Cut the stem and root part from the top and bottom of the onions, then peel off the dry skin. Chop the onions into small pieces and place in a small bowl.
2. Slice the hot dogs into disks, each about as thick as your pinkie finger.
3. Place the sliced hot dogs in the cook pot. Add the chili from the cans to the pot.

4. You'll need a heat source of about medium strength. Too hot, and it will burn. Stir occasionally with a spoon until the chili dog mixture is warm. This will take about 5 minutes.
5. Arrange 8 plates and set a hot dog bun on each. Using clean hands, open each bun and mash it flat!

6. Use a spoon or a ladle to cover each of the buns with some of the chili dog mixture. Top the chili with the chopped onions, if desired, then add a handful of shredded cheese.
7. You won't be able to easily eat this chili dog with your fingers, so plan to pass out forks.

Servings: 8

Preparation time: 30 minutes

Poor Man's Stew

1 pound lean ground beef
1 (10.75-ounce) can condensed
   tomato soup
2 (10.75-ounce) cans condensed
   alphabet soup
1 (15-ounce) can mixed vegetables

EQUIPMENT:

Large cook pot
Long-handled wooden spoon
Can opener
Ladle

PREPARATION:

1. Put the ground beef in the cook pot and place the pot on the heat source. If you're using a stove, cook this meal on medium.
2. Use a wooden spoon to constantly stir and break up the chunks of meat. Cook until the beef is no longer pink. If it begins to burn, reduce the heat.
3. Pour the cans of tomato soup and alphabet soup into the pot.
4. Add the can of mixed vegetables, including the juice, to the pot.
5. Stir the stew well, then reduce the heat to low. Occasionally stir the stew until it is hot.
6. Serve the stew with a ladle.

Servings: 6–8
Preparation time: 30 minutes

MARC DUFRESNE

How Many Servings?

By now you've noticed that every recipe, at the end, suggests how many people the recipe will serve. We could be wrong. If everyone is really hungry, the recipe might serve less people. If no one is really hungry, it might serve more.

Don't Cook in Your Tent!

On a cold, windy, rainy day it might be tempting to cook in your tent using a stove or other cooking equipment, but don't! Why?

The first and most obvious problem is that cooking in a tent can cause your tent or gear to melt or catch fire.

The second concern is invisible. Fuels like gas, wood, charcoal, and propane release a poison called carbon monoxide. Outdoors, this gas dissipates into the air and is usually not a problem. But in an enclosed tent this gas can build up and make you very sick. Carbon monoxide poisoning can cause shortness of breath, headaches, confusion, dizziness, loss of consciousness, or even death. Carbon monoxide has no smell, so you won't know it's a problem until it's too late. This is why you should never cook in your tent!

Frying

Frying is cooking food in hot oil (or another kind of fat). In a deep pot full of oil, it's called deep-frying. In a shallow pan, it's called, no surprise, shallow-frying. In this book, we are not going to do any deep-frying for a couple of reasons. One reason: oil is highly flammable, which means potentially dangerous, especially over a fire. Another reason: oil is heavy and messy, and when you are finished deep-frying, you have to figure out what to do with the oil. So, let's stick with a pan, a little bit of oil, and shallow-frying.

By the way, as food fries, some of the oil in the pan will be absorbed by the food. That's a good thing for most people because most people think the oil adds flavor.

EMS-FORESTER-PRODUCTIONS

This is important. When you're shallow-frying, you need to flip whatever you're frying at least once. So if you plan on frying, bring a spatula. If you don't flip, you'll end up with the bottom side (of the food) burned before the top side is ready to eat.

It's amazingly easy to burn food in a hot frying pan. One reason is the pan gets hotter and hotter the longer it sits on the heat source. That's one reason to let a campfire burn down to hot coals before you cook. You can spread the coals out to reduce the heat. You can also carefully lift the frying pan off the heat until it cools off—then put it back on to finish cooking. It's a lot easier when you're frying on a stove. Just turn the heat down.

Many foods can be fried, including meat, potatoes, vegetables, cheese, and even grasshoppers. To be an all-around great outdoor cook, you will do well to learn to fry—even if you prefer to avoid grasshoppers.

Beware of Hot Oil

Water boils at 212°F, and after that the water doesn't get much hotter. But oil can get a lot hotter than 212°F. Some oils can get hotter than 500°F! And so it can burn you faster and deeper. See "Don't Get Burned" in the introduction for how to treat burns.

Water and Oil Don't Mix

Most of the time, before you throw something in a frying pan, it's best to dry it off. Wet food in a hot pan sputters and splatters, and the hot oil can fly out and burn you. In fact, here's a good idea: keep water away from hot oil.

HXYUME

FRYING RECIPES

Sausage and Egg Burritos

1 pound precooked frozen sausage patties
Cooking spray
6 eggs
6 (8-inch) flour tortillas
1 (16-ounce) jar salsa (Mild, medium, hot? It's up to you.)

EQUIPMENT:

Medium-size frying pan
Long-handled spoon

JASMIN MERDAN

PREPARATION:

1. Precooked sausage patties come in a variety of types and sizes. The number of patties isn't important for this recipe, but the weight is. Set aside about 1 pound of patties if the package contains more than this amount.

2. The sausage must be thawed. If the patties have been in a cooler overnight, they shouldn't need more than about 30 to 60 minutes to soften unless the morning temperature is cold. If the patties are frozen or the air temperature cold, seal them in a Ziploc bag and set the bag in warm water for about 15 minutes.

3. Spray the inside of the frying pan with cooking spray.

4. Crumble the sausage patties into the pan. The pieces of sausage should be bite-size, not too large.

5. Crack the eggs over the sausage.

6. Place the frying pan on the heat source. You want medium heat for this.

7. Stir the sausage and eggs together using the spoon. Keep stirring while the eggs cook, to keep the food from burning.

8. Take the pan off the heat once the eggs are ready. The eggs are fully cooked when there is no clear, runny liquid remaining and they are yellow throughout.

9. Lay a tortilla flat on a serving plate. Scoop some of the sausage-egg mixture onto the tortilla. You'll need enough of the sausage-egg mixture for 6 tortillas, so try not to use too much or too little.

10. Top the sausage and eggs with a couple tablespoons of salsa, then roll the tortilla like you would a burrito by tucking the sides in, then rolling like a carpet.

11. Repeat the laying out, filling, and rolling for the remaining 5 tortillas.

Servings: 6
Preparation time: 30 minutes

Very Berry Pancakes

1 cup frozen blueberries

2 cups Aunt Jemima Original Complete pancake and waffle mix
   (or something similar)

1½ cups water

¼ cup (½ standard stick) butter

¼ cup confectioners' sugar (aka "powdered sugar")

Maple syrup (as much as you want—unless someone yells "Stop!")

EQUIPMENT:

Large mixing bowl

Long-handled spoon

Medium-sized frying pan

Spatula

JUPITERIMAGES

PREPARATION:

1. Pour the pancake mix into a large bowl, then add the water to the bowl. Mix well with a spoon until no large lumps remain in the batter.
2. Add the blueberries to the batter and stir gently.
3. Melt 1 tablespoon (about a 1-inch chunk) of butter in the frying pan over low to medium heat.
4. Move the butter around with the spoon while it melts to cover all the inside of the pan. If the butter starts to sizzle, the pan is too hot, so reduce the heat.
5. Pour some batter into the hot frying pan. Using a measuring cup can make this step easier. Be sure to scoop up some of the blueberries too, because they tend to sink to the bottom of the batter in the bowl. Pour just enough batter to make a cake about 6 inches in diameter. The batter will spread out after you pour it, so don't put too much into the pan. Until you get used to making pancakes, cook only one at a time.
6. Once many bubbles appear on the top of the pancake, use a spatula to quickly flip the pancake over. Practice makes perfect with this step!
7. Cook for only a short period of time on the second side. Usually about a minute is all that's needed.
8. Move the pancake to a serving plate, then repeat the last three steps—pouring some batter into the pan and cooking the pancake on both sides—until all the batter is used up. Melt more butter in the pan as it's used up.
9. Sprinkle confectioners' sugar over the pancakes when serving. Cover with maple syrup.

Servings: 6–8
Preparation time: 45 minutes

Fry Bread

1 cup self-rising flour, plus a little extra for working the dough
1 teaspoon Italian seasoning blend
½ teaspoon garlic salt
½ cup water
3 tablespoons olive oil

EQUIPMENT:

Medium-sized frying pan
Spatula
Medium-sized bowl

SERGEY DROZD/500PX

PREPARATION:

1. Combine 1 cup flour, Italian seasoning, garlic salt, and water in a bowl. Mix well.
2. Warm the oil over medium heat in the frying pan.
3. With floured hands, create 4 dough balls of roughly equal size, place in the pan, and flatten with a spatula.
4. Fry on one side. Flip. Fry on other side until both sides are golden brown.

Servings: 4
Preparation time: 30 minutes

Campfire Potatoes

2 pounds skin-on red or new
    potatoes, washed
3 tablespoons extra virgin olive oil
1 tablespoon minced fresh rosemary
2 cloves garlic, minced
Salt to taste

EQUIPMENT:

Large frying pan
Spatula

VISUALSPACE

PREPARATION:

1. Cut the potatoes into ¾-inch
   bite-size chunks.
2. Warm the oil in the frying pan over medium heat, then add the rosemary, garlic, salt, and potatoes.
3. Fry the potatoes, stirring occasionally, until crispy on the outside and
   soft on the inside.

Servings: 4–6
Preparation time: 30 minutes

Texas BBQ Sandwich

2 ounces sliced ham sandwich meat
2 ounces sliced turkey sandwich meat
1 slice Swiss cheese
2 slices bread
1 tablespoon BBQ sauce
¼ tablespoon butter, softened
Optional: mustard to taste

EQUIPMENT:

Medium-sized frying pan with lid
Spatula

WESTEND61

PREPARATION:

1. Lay the meat and cheese on one of the bread slices.
2. Spread barbecue sauce on one side of the second slice of bread.
3. Cover the cheese and meat with the second slice of bread, barbecue sauce facing the meat and cheese.
4. Butter the outside face of each slice of bread.
5. Fry the sandwich in a covered frying pan over low heat, lightly toasting each side before serving with optional mustard.

Servings: 1
Preparation time: 15 minutes

Sloppy Joes

1 pound lean ground beef
1 tablespoon mustard
½ cup ketchup
¼ cup brown sugar
6 hamburger buns

EQUIPMENT:

Medium-sized frying pan
Long-handled spoon

PREPARATION:

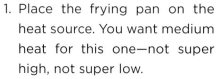

FILADENDRON

1. Place the frying pan on the heat source. You want medium heat for this one—not super high, not super low.
2. Add the ground beef to the pan and begin breaking apart the lumps with the spoon. Keep stirring as the pan becomes hot, to keep the beef from burning.
3. Continue to break apart the lumps of beef while stirring. Once the meat has become gray in color with no hint of pink remaining (this is important to make sure it's fully cooked), add the yellow mustard and the ketchup to the pan. Stir everything well with the spoon.
4. Add the brown sugar to the beef and stir until well mixed. Cook for another minute, then remove the pan from the heat.
5. Serve the sloppy joe mixture on buns. This can be a pretty messy business. It's easier to place a single bun on a plate first, open it, and then scoop some of the beef mixture onto the bottom half with a spoon.

Servings: 6
Preparation time: 30 minutes

Quesadillas

1 bell pepper, any color

1 medium-sized onion

1 (4-ounce) can sliced black olives

1 (16-ounce) can refried beans

1 (8-ounce) package shredded cheese, your choice

10 large flour tortillas

Vegetable oil for greasing frying pan

Optional: sour cream, salsa

EQUIPMENT:

Medium-sized frying pan

Knife

Can opener

3 small bowls

2 medium-sized bowls

5 serving spoons

Spatula

YULIYA TABA

PREPARATION:

1. Remove the top stem part from the bell pepper. Cut the pepper in half, remove the seeds, then scrape out the white "ribs" on the inside. Chop what's left of the pepper into small pieces and place them in a small bowl.

2. Cut the stem and root part from the top and bottom of the onion, then peel off the dry skin. Also peel off the first layer of the onion under the dry skin. Chop up the onion and place it in a second small bowl.

3. Drain the liquid from the can of sliced olives. (If the olives are whole, slice them into smaller pieces.) Put the olives into a third small bowl.

4. Open the can of refried beans and scoop them into a medium-sized bowl.

5. Pour the shredded cheese into another medium-sized bowl.

6. Place a serving spoon in each of the bowls.

7. Everyone who wants to eat needs a plate with a tortilla on it. Have the diners cover the tortillas with their choice of ingredients from the bowls.

8. Spread the ingredients evenly over the tortilla but leave some room around the edge. Place a second tortilla over the ingredients and press lightly to squash it down.

9. Warm the frying pan over the heat source. Add about 1 tablespoon of vegetable oil to the pan and spread it around with a spatula.

10. Place a quesadilla (the two tortillas with the food between them) gently in the warm pan. Cook until the bottom is browned, then flip the quesadilla and cook on the other side until that tortilla is browned. The cheese, now partly melted, will hold the quesadilla together. If the tortilla begins to smoke, reduce the heat.

11. Remove the quesadilla from the frying pan to a serving plate, then cook the next one. Cook only one at a time. Add more oil to the pan if it begins to dry out.

12. Serve with optional sour cream and salsa. The quesadillas can be cut in half for smaller stomachs.

Servings: 5–10 (depending on hunger)
Preparation time: 1 hour

Corn Cakes

1 (8.5-ounce) package Jiffy corn
    muffin mix (or something similar)
1 egg
⅓ cup milk
2 tablespoons butter

EQUIPMENT:

Quart-size Ziploc bag
Medium-sized frying pan
Spatula
Scissors or small knife

PREPARATION:

1. Pour the corn muffin mix into a quart-sized Ziploc bag.
2. Ask someone to hold the bag while you crack the egg into it and then add the milk.
3. Seal the bag tightly while squeezing the air out, then carefully squish the ingredients together in the bag until all the large lumps are gone.
4. Place the frying pan on the heat source. You don't want a lot of heat. Go for low medium. Melt the butter in the warm frying pan, then spread the melted butter around using a spatula.

5. Pinch a bottom corner of the Ziploc bag to move the muffin batter out of it, then cut the corner off using a pair of scissors or a small knife. The corner cut should be about ½ inch long.
6. Squirt some of the batter out of the bag's corner cut into the hot frying pan like you might do for pancakes. Form as many corn cakes as will fit in the pan, but keep them at least an inch apart from each other at first, because the batter will expand.

7. Once the corn cakes begin to bubble slightly, flip them with the spatula onto their other side, then cook for a minute or two before removing them from the pan.

8. Continue cooking any remaining batter the same way until the batter is used up.

Servings: 4–6
Preparation time: 30 minutes

Don't Feed the Animals!

It can be hard to resist feeding those adorable little critters who sometimes visit your picnic table. But there are several good reasons why we don't want to feed the animals:

- Feeding animals can cause them to become dependent on human food (which is often unhealthy for them).
- Animals can lose their natural ability to find their own food.
- Wild animals sometimes carry diseases that can be transmitted to humans.
- Attracting large animals like bears is clearly just dangerous!

Store food and trash so animals can't get it.

Use bear lockers when available!

In bear country look for bear lockers (secure food boxes) and bear-proof trash cans. Some people store their food in their cars, but watch out because in areas where lots of tourists meet lots of bears (like Yosemite National Park), bears are known to regularly break into cars looking for food.

DOUGLAS SACHA

A bear-proof trash bin

Bear bagging is one way to keep animals and bears from getting your food.

Bear bagging is one way to keep food away from animals. Hang your food, trash, and other smelly items like toothpaste in this bag as well.

Bear-proof canisters work well for storing smaller amounts of food.

Grilling

If you've been paying attention (which is a very important thing to do), you know that when you boil food the heat source makes the water hot, and the heat of the water cooks the food. When you fry, the heat source makes the oil hot. When you grill, the heat cooks the food directly. There's no water, pan, or pot in between. What is between the heat and food is an open grate, a series of metal bars that may run parallel to each other or may cross over each other.

There's a good chance you have a grill in your backyard. The grill stands above the heat source when you're cooking outdoors, the meat or vegetables or both go on the metal bars, and pretty soon your food is cooked.

This fire pit comes with a fold-down grate.

YELLOW DOG PRODUCTIONS

Many campgrounds have fire pits with a grill attached. For sale are collapsible grills (sometimes called grates) that are sturdy and easy to use. When the fire has burned down to hot coals, you just pop the legs out on the grate and set it over the heat. You can also use pots and pans on a grate—which means with a grate you can boil and fry as well as grill.

Note: You do not want a raging fire under a grill. You want a bed of hot coals that you can push together to increase heat or spread out to reduce heat.

GRILLING RECIPES

Backwoods Chicken

1 egg
1 cup vegetable oil
2 cups cider vinegar
3 tablespoons salt
1 tablespoon poultry seasoning
1 teaspoon ground black pepper
12 chicken drumsticks or thighs

EQUIPMENT:

Medium-sized mixing bowl
2 gallon-sized Ziploc plastic bags or
large covered bowl
Tongs, long ones

PREPARATION:

1. In a medium-sized bowl, beat the egg, then add the remaining ingredients except the chicken. Blend well.
2. Place the chicken in the Ziploc bag or large bowl. Pour the egg marinade over the chicken. Allow the chicken to absorb the marinade for at least 1 hour, preferably longer, in a chilled cooler.
3. Remove the chicken pieces from the marinade and arrange on the grill over high heat. Every 5 to 10 minutes, turn the chicken with tongs and baste with more marinade.
4. Cook until a fork can easily pierce the flesh, revealing no remaining trace of pink meat (or to a temperature of 165°F).

Servings: 12
Preparation time: ½ to 1 hour

Juicy Worm Burgers

This recipe puts a fun spin on plain old hamburgers and is sure to make every-one at camp giggle and squirm. The juice from the meat swells the noodles while grilling, causing them to hang out of the burgers like juicy worms!

1 pound ground beef
½ cup dried chow mein noodles
Salt and ground black
    pepper to taste
4 hamburger buns
Toppings: cheese, tomatoes,
    lettuce, onions, ketchup,
    mayonnaise, mustard—
    you choose

EQUIPMENT:

Medium-sized mixing bowl
Long-handled spatula

PREPARATION:

1. Combine the beef and chow mein noodles in the bowl. Add salt and black pepper.
2. Gently knead the ingredients to combine, then form mixture into 4 patties.
3. Grill the burgers to your desired level of doneness, flipping them a couple of times, and serve on buns with toppings of choice.

JUANMONINO

Servings: 4
Preparation time: 30 minutes

Veggies with Goat Cheese

1 pound fresh whole mushrooms, sliced in half
1 large red onion, sliced into ½-inch-thick disks
2 tablespoons olive oil, plus a little extra
1 tablespoon Italian seasoning mix
½ teaspoon salt
½ teaspoon ground black pepper
1 pint grape tomatoes
4 ounces crumbled goat cheese

EQUIPMENT:

Medium-sized mixing bowl
Grill basket
Paper towel

NATHAN BLANEY

Grill baskets make grilling vegetables easy.

PREPARATION:

1. Combine the mushrooms, onion, olive oil, Italian seasoning, salt, and black pepper in the bowl. Toss to mix.
2. Place a little olive oil on a paper towel and wipe the oil over the grill basket. This will prevent the vegetables from sticking to the basket.
3. Place the vegetable mix in the grill basket and cook over embers or low flame for about 10 minutes, until the onions soften.
4. Shake the basket to mix the veggies, then add the tomatoes. Continue to cook for an additional 5 minutes.
5. Return the cooked vegetables to the bowl and add goat cheese. Toss.
6. Allow the cheese to melt for a couple of minutes before serving.

Servings: 6–8
Preparation time: 30 minutes

Mexican Campfire Corn

4 ears fresh corn, shucked

½ cup Mexican crema (it's sort
of like sour cream)

1 teaspoon chili powder

½ cup crumbled queso fresco
(a special white cheese)

1 lime, juiced

EQUIPMENT:

4 metal skewers, long and strong

PREPARATION:

1. Carefully insert a skewer into the cob end of each of the ears of corn.
2. Grill the corn for about 10 minutes, turning frequently until slightly charred.
3. Remove the corn from the grill. Brush each ear with Mexican crema, then sprinkle with chili powder, queso fresco, and lime juice.

Servings: 4
Preparation time: 20 minutes

IPPEI NAOI

Baking

When you bake something, you almost always use dry heat (little or no water) and an enclosed space (usually called an oven). Of all baked goods, bread is the oldest and most famous. But today you're far more likely to think of cookies and cakes. If you can bake it at home, you can bake it outdoors.

Great food can be baked in a Dutch oven, and, if you keep reading this book, you'll find out about that. Also, you can bake by using a reflector oven near your campfire. Once again, you need to keep reading. You can even make your own oven: a box oven. And, yes, you'll find out all about a box oven soon.

You can bake by putting a rock near your fire and, when the rock gets hot, placing something on it to cook. You can also bake by putting something in the hot ashes of a campfire. We are not going to recommend hot rocks and hot ashes in this book because, honestly, we don't like the results very much. You can even bake on a stick. And we do like that, so you'll find how to do it in the chapter "Cooking on a 'Stick.'"

REFLECTOR OVEN

Reflector ovens are a fun way to bake in the wild. They are usually pretty light, typically weighing a few pounds, and require only a simple campfire to get them working. (Yes, a fire, so if you're not careful, it's easy to get a nasty burn!) By facing the opening of your oven toward the campfire, the heat from your campfire makes its way to the shiny metal in the back of your oven where it  bounces the heat onto your food. This heat will bake almost anything that fits in your oven—bread, pies, and cookies, for example.

You can bake a blueberry pie in your reflector oven!

Things to think about:

1. You're going to need some heavy gloves to move the hot oven around.
2. When putting the pieces of your oven together, make sure the shiniest sides of the metal face inward. This will ensure the oven reflects the maximum amount of heat onto your food.
3. Never put the oven on top of an open fire, grill, or coals! Place your oven close enough to the fire that it captures its heat but far enough away that it's not burning your food. The ideal distance between the oven and fire will depend on the size of your fire, so have gloves ready to move the oven closer or farther away as the fire naturally changes.
4. Because of the fickle nature of fires, you will need to watch your food carefully to make sure that it's cooking and not burning. To ensure even cooking, turn the food inside your oven frequently using gloves.

BOX OVEN

The box oven is a simple and reliable way to bake outdoors. It is easy to build and use. There are different ways to make a box oven, but this one is our favorite because it's so easy!

ALLISON RUDICK

English muffin pizzas baked in a box oven

ALLISON RUDICK

What you'll need:

17 × 11-inch empty cardboard copy paper box (the kind used for holding 10 reams of copy paper)

Heavy-duty 18-inch-wide roll of aluminum foil

Duct tape

4 small, flat rocks or similar fireproof objects

4 empty, clean 15-ounce cans, labels removed, all of the exact same size

13 × 9-inch cookie sheet

1 small brick or similar-sized rock

Bag of briquettes (there's lots of info on briquettes in the Dutch oven section)

Heavy gloves

Long-handled tongs

Building your box oven:

1. Remove the lid of the box and set it aside. You will use it again to help transport and store the items in your box.

2. Tear off a long sheet of foil and push it down into the inside of the box so that the sheet runs the long length of the box. Press the foil tightly into the corners, with the edges of the foil coming up the side walls on the inside of the box. The sheet should be long enough to come up and over the walls at both ends of the box.

ALLISON RUDICK

3. Run a second long sheet of foil across the narrow width of the box, pressing it into the corners and up and over the walls. The sides of the sheet of foil should overlap the first foil sheet, with all foil now pressed against the walls. Be certain that no cardboard is exposed!

ALLISON RUDICK

4. Fold any extra foil over the edge and tape it onto the outside of the box using duct tape. The outside of the box does not need to be completely covered in foil. Don't use tape inside the box!

ALLISON RUDICK

Cooking in your new box oven:

1. Tear off a sheet of wide foil longer than the length of the box. Lay this sheet of foil on level ground, free of debris, in your fire-safe zone. Set a small, flat rock or similar fireproof weight on each of the 4 corners of the foil.

2. Arrange the 4 empty cans in a rectangle on the foil, with the open ends pointing down. Space them so that each one will hold up one corner of the cookie sheet.

ALLISON RUDICK

3. Place the cookie tray on the tops of the empty cans. If the tray is unstable, rearrange the cans to improve stability. Be sure the tray is level.

ALLISON RUDICK

4. Set the box upside-down over the cookie tray. Reposition the 4 rocks so each one is under a corner of the box, to hold the box slightly off the ground. This will allow oxygen to reach the burning coals.

ALLISON RUDICK

5. With all the pieces in position and ready to go, remove the box until it's time to cook.
6. Time to fire up the briquettes! How many? With 9 briquettes, your oven will reach about 360°F. At 360°, you can bake just about anything.
7. If you aren't sure what temperature would be best for a particular dish, 360°F is a good place to start. You can take briquettes out, using long-handled tongs, if you think it's too hot, but, for safety reasons, do not exceed 360° (9 briquettes) in your box oven. If you need to move hot briquettes, ask an adult for help.

Note: As briquettes burn, they become smaller and produce less heat. You may need to fire up more briquettes depending on the weather conditions and the length of time it normally takes to make your dish. Remember that every time you open your oven, heat escapes and the temperature of the oven drops.

ALLISON RUDICK

Coals being prepared in a Coal Chimney Starter

8. Spread the hot coals evenly on the sheet of foil on the ground. Distribute them within the perimeter formed by the empty cans. Don't place them where they will be too close to the edges of the box once it's in place.

ALLISON RUDICK

9. Place the cookie sheet on top of the cans, then set the item you're baking, such as a pan of prepared brownie batter, on the cookie sheet.

ALLISON RUDICK

10. Place the box over the item you're baking. Be sure that the rocks are under the corners of the box to provide proper ventilation. If it's windy, you can place a small rock on top of the box to give it stability.

ALLISON RUDICK

11. Time the cooking according to the recipe instructions you are following. Once ready to serve, the box will be very hot! When removing the box, do so only while wearing protective gloves.

ALLISON RUDICK

12. When you're done cooking, make sure your coals are completely cool. When the items are no longer hot, put them back into the box and cover with the lid for transport.

ALLISON RUDICK

Safety tips:

- Before baking food in your box oven for the first time, take it on a test drive. In a fire-safe area, use 9 briquettes under the cookie sheet, distributed as if you were actually baking food. Set the box over the coals with proper ventilation and allow the coals to expire on their own, about an hour or so. Remove the box and then carefully examine it, inside and out, for any sign of burn damage or weakening, which would likely be due to a lack of foil or a gap between the foil sheets. Correct any deficiencies before using the oven in the field.

- The aluminum foil helps to protect the cardboard by reflecting heat, but don't use more than 9 coals to help ensure that the temperature inside the box always stays below the ignition point for paper. Using more than 9 coals can also cause the cardboard to warp. Never allow coals to come into direct contact with the box.

- Be sure that your oven is in good repair before using it in the field. Ensure that it's only operated in a fire-safe area, and keep it away from low-hanging branches, fuel, or other combustibles. Have plenty of water on hand to douse flames should it become necessary.

SOLAR OVEN

Solar ovens use the energy of the sun to cook your food! You can purchase a solar oven or build your own. It's not necessarily the most efficient or predictable way to cook your food, but it's definitely a ton of fun! Here are the instructions for building a solar oven using an old pizza box.

What you'll need:

Large pizza box (approximately
   9½ × 9½ inches and
   2 inches deep)
Marker or pen
Ruler
Sharp kitchen knife or box cutter
Plastic wrap
Clear packaging tape

Aluminum foil
Elmer's-style glue
Black paper
Newspaper
Short stick or pencil
Scissors
Pie pan or shallow container
Optional: cooking thermometer

Building your solar oven:

1. Use a marker and ruler to create three lines about 1 inch in from each edge of the top of the pizza box. No line is needed at the hinge (back) of the box.

ALLISON RUDICK

2. With the help of an adult, carefully cut out the front and sides of the top of the pizza box. Leave the hinge side uncut.

ALLISON RUDICK

ALLISON RUDICK

3. You should have created a door/flap on top of your pizza box.

4. Seal the opening with plastic wrap. Tape all edges of the wrap onto the inside lid of the box and make sure it's airtight. The plastic window will allow direct and reflected sunlight (light that bounces off the foil) to enter the box and hold in the heat.

ALLISON RUDICK

5. Glue aluminum foil onto the inside of the "door" with the foil shiny side out. The less wrinkled it is, the better it will reflect. Fold any excess foil behind the door and glue in place. The foil on the door will be used to reflect sunlight onto the food in your pizza box. Line the entire bottom of the inside of the box with foil. Glue in place.

ALLISON RUDICK

ALLISON RUDICK

6. Place black paper over the foil on the bottom of the oven and glue in place. The color black absorbs all wavelengths of light and converts them into thermal energy or heat. This will help your solar oven get hotter.

ALLISON RUDICK

7. Your finished oven should look something like this!

ALLISON RUDICK

Cooking in your new solar oven:

1. Place the food in a pie pan or shallow container that will fit inside your closed oven. Place this container on top of the black paper inside the box. You can help insulate your oven by rolling newspaper into tubes and stuffing them around the dish to help hold onto the heat.

2. Close the pizza box lid but keep the flap or door open. You can use a stick or a pencil to hold up the flap and adjust its angle to help direct the reflected light onto your food.

ALLISON RUDICK

Canned ravioli heated by the sun

3. Place your oven in a way that best reflects the sun's light from the foil flap onto the food inside the window of your box. You can expect to make some adjustments to your pizza box and flap as the sun moves across the sky. Frequently check to make sure that sunlight is being directed back into your box.

Things to consider:

- Because it's a solar oven, you'll need to wait for a sunny day and as you probably already guessed, you can't use it at night. In fact, the best time to cook is between 11:00 a.m. and 3:00 p.m., when the sun is directly overhead. If you start too late in the day, the sun might set before your dish is done.

- The outside temperature shouldn't matter too much, but you might want to avoid windy days that could cause your oven to take off like a kite.

- Most homemade solar ovens can reach about 200°F plus. This is a relatively low temperature that is usually only good for warming your food, and you'll need to be patient as even warming your food might take a while.

- Cooking times in a solar oven are unpredictable because they depend entirely on the availability of the sun. For that reason, we recommend using your solar oven only for dishes that can be safely eaten uncooked and only require reheating or melting. Making s'mores or mini pizzas and heating a can of chili are examples of fail-proof uses for your oven. Trying to cook raw meat is not a good idea.

Dutch Oven Cooking

SCOTT SIMERLY

An oven is something you put food in to cook when heat is applied. A Dutch oven is the simplest of ovens. It's a cast-iron pot with thick sides and a snug-fitting lid. A snug lid is important because it traps heat and sometimes moisture inside the pot for efficient cooking. And a big bonus: it's more than just an oven! You can fry and boil in a Dutch oven too. If it's made especially for cooking outdoors, the Dutch oven could have legs. The legs make it easier to use a Dutch oven over coals or briquettes.

You can bake bread in a Dutch oven!

Briquettes

You may have noticed that several cooking methods in this book rely on coal briquettes. A briquette is a block of compressed charcoal used as fuel for outdoor cooking. Briquettes are often used in grilling, cooking on a stick, and foil cooking, but they can be particularly useful in Dutch oven cooking. This is because, unlike the unpredictable nature of burning wood and embers, each briquette releases a fairly predictable (even) amount of heat. This allows you more control over the temperatures in a Dutch oven.

Briquettes can be tricky to fire up. A lot of people like to pour lighter fluid on them, then set a match to the briquettes. This can cause a big poof of flames, so never light briquettes without an adult watching.

Charcoal Chimney Starter

Things to think about when cooking with briquettes:

1. When baking, briquettes are placed on both the top and the bottom of the oven. Because heat rises, we typically put fewer briquettes on the bottom of the oven than the top to avoid burning our food.
2. Always work in a fire-safe area away from debris and tents.
3. Use protective gear, such as heavy gloves and long-handled tongs, when moving hot coals. If the gloves are long enough to protect your lower arms, that's a really good thing.
4. Wear closed-top shoes when working with briquettes.
5. Never use briquettes inside a tent or camper.
6. The amount of heat each briquette produces can vary depending on the size or brand you use.
7. Bring extra charcoal briquettes. Food preparation may take longer than expected, so you'll need more briquettes. Windy, cold, or wet weather can also greatly increase the number of coals required. Don't get caught with an empty bag of briquettes and an oven of half-baked food!

Never work with coals without adult supervision! Grilling gloves should be worn when working with coals. Tongs can be used to move coals into position.

DUTCH OVEN RECIPES

SCOTT SIMERLY

Breakfast Casserole

1 pound uncooked Italian sausage,
   casings removed
6 eggs
2 cups milk
1 teaspoon salt
½ teaspoon ground mustard
6 slices bread, torn into small pieces
1 cup shredded cheddar cheese
Ground black pepper to taste

EQUIPMENT:

10-inch Dutch oven
Medium-sized mixing bowl

PREPARATION:

1. In a Dutch oven preheated over 21 coals, brown the sausage.
2. Remove the Dutch oven from the coals, then carefully drain the grease into an empty can or unused pot. Set the oven aside for a moment.
3. Beat the eggs in a bowl, then add milk, salt, and ground mustard.
4. Stir the bread pieces and cheese into the egg mixture.
5. Pour the egg-bread mixture over the sausage in the Dutch oven.
6. Cover the oven and move 14 briquettes to the lid, leaving 7 under the oven.
7. Bake for about 40 minutes, refreshing the coals if required, until the eggs set. Serve with black pepper to taste.

Servings: 6–8
Preparation time: 1 hour and 15 minutes

Quiche

This recipe can be prepared in a Dutch oven, box oven, or reflector oven!

1 (9-inch) deep-dish frozen piecrust
    that comes in a reusable pan
2 green onions
1 (7-ounce) can Spam
4 eggs
1 cup milk
1 cup shredded cheddar cheese

EQUIPMENT:

10-inch Dutch oven
Aluminum foil
Knife

Large mixing bowl
Long-handled spoon

1. Remove the premade piecrust from the cooler but leave it in the pan it comes in.
2. Prepare 25 briquettes for the Dutch oven, then preheat the oven using 8 coals underneath and 17 coals on the lid.

3. Cut the ragged top parts from the green onions. Remove the stringy roots too. Chop the rest of the green onions into pieces.
4. Open the can of Spam and drain the liquid into the trash. Remove the Spam from the can, then chop the meat into small cubes. The cubes should be about the size of dice—maybe a bit smaller.

5. Crack the eggs into the large bowl.
6. To the bowl with the eggs, add the milk, shredded cheddar cheese, chopped green onions, and chopped Spam. Stir all the ingredients together with the spoon.
7. Carefully pour the mixture containing the eggs and Spam into the pie-crust shell.

8. It's time now to be very careful! Remove the hot lid from the Dutch oven.
9. Roll about two feet of aluminum foil into a "snake." Coil the snake in the bottom of the oven. You don't want the pie pan to sit directly on the bottom of the oven. Some type of metal trivet will work here too.

10. Carefully set the filled pie pan on the foil snake or trivet in the oven.
11. Replace the lid, ensuring an even distribution of 17 coals on the lid and 8 under the oven.
12. Bake for about 30 minutes, until the eggs have become firm.

13. Remove the pie pan from the oven with gloves (careful!) and allow the quiche to cool for about 10 minutes before serving.

Servings: 6–8
Preparation time: 1 hour

Pirate's Catch

Cooking spray
1 (6-ounce) package cornbread
    stuffing mix
1½ cups water
¼ cup (½ standard stick) butter
2 pounds white fish fillets (tilapia,
    flounder, trout, sole, haddock,
    cod, or pollock)
2 lemons

EQUIPMENT:

10-inch Dutch oven
Long-handled spoon
Knife

PREPARATION:

1. Prepare 21 briquettes for the Dutch oven.
2. Spray the inside of the Dutch oven with cooking spray.
3. Dump the stuffing mix into the Dutch oven.
4. Pour the water over the stuffing mix and stir well with the spoon.
5. Slice the butter into thin pieces. Lay the butter slices over the stuffing mixture.
6. Lay the fish fillets over the butter and stuffing mixture.
7. Slice the lemons into thin circles and lay them over the fish fillets.
8. Put the lid on the oven. Place 7 coals under the oven and 14 coals on the lid.
9. Bake for about 40 minutes.
10. Check to be sure the fish is fully cooked before serving. It should pull apart easily.

Servings: 6–8
Preparation time: 1 hour

Dutch Oven Fiesta

1 medium-sized onion
1 pound lean ground beef
1 (1.25-ounce) package taco seasoning mix
1 (14.5-ounce) can diced tomatoes with green chilies
1 (15-ounce) can sweet corn
2 eggs
⅔ cup milk
2 (8.5-ounce) packages Jiffy corn muffin mix

EQUIPMENT:

10-inch Dutch oven
Knife
Long-handled spoon
Can opener
Medium-sized bowl
Fork

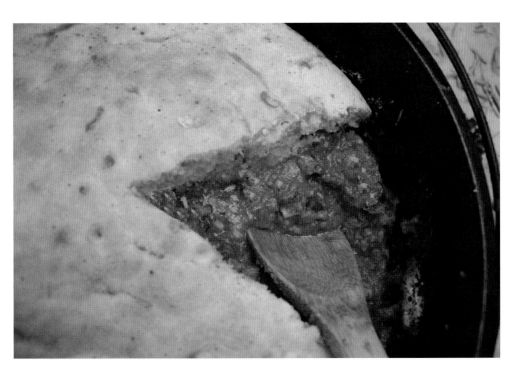

PREPARATION:

1. Warm the Dutch oven over 21 coals.
2. Cut the stem and root part from the top and bottom of the onion, then peel off the dry skin. Chop the onion into pieces.
3. Carefully place the chopped onion in the hot Dutch oven.
4. Add the ground beef to the Dutch oven and begin breaking apart the lumps with the spoon. Stir the beef, mixing it with the onions.
5. Continue to break apart the lumps of beef while stirring often. Once the meat has become gray with no hint of pink remaining, add the package of taco seasoning. Stir well.
6. Add the can of tomatoes with green chilies to the oven.
7. Drain the juice from the can of sweet corn and pour the corn into the oven. Stir everything again.
8. Crack the eggs into the medium-sized bowl. Mix them by stirring very quickly with a fork, then add the milk to the eggs and stir again.
9. Pour both packages of corn muffin mix into the bowl of eggs and milk. Stir well with the spoon until the batter is thick and no large lumps remain.
10. Use the spoon to scoop the batter out of the bowl and onto the beef mixture in the oven. Don't stir the batter into the beef mixture, just put it on top!
11. Place the lid on the oven, then move 14 coals from under the oven to the lid. Leave the other 7 below.
12. Bake for about 30 minutes. The muffin mix is cooked when you can insert a knife into it and it comes out clean.

Servings: 6–8
Preparation time: 1 hour

BBQ Meatloaf

1 pound frozen mixed vegetables, your choice

1 pound lean ground beef

¼ cup dried minced onions

1 cup unseasoned dried breadcrumbs

2 eggs

1 (15- to 18-ounce) bottle barbecue sauce

Salt and ground black pepper to taste

EQUIPMENT:

10-inch Dutch oven

Medium-sized mixing bowl

Spatula

LAURIPATTERSON

PREPARATION:

1. About an hour before starting the coals, set the mixed vegetables out to thaw if they are still frozen.
2. Prepare 21 briquettes for the Dutch oven.
3. Put the ground beef into the mixing bowl.
4. Pour the dried minced onions into the bowl, then add the breadcrumbs.
5. Crack the eggs into the bowl, then add ¼ cup of barbecue sauce.
6. Use clean hands to mush the ingredients in the bowl together until everything is evenly blended.
7. Form the meat mixture into a shape that resembles a small loaf of bread. Keep in mind that it will need to fit into the Dutch oven without touching the walls.
8. Set the meatloaf in the middle of the Dutch oven, keeping it away from the walls. Make sure the loaf won't touch the inside of the lid once the lid is on the oven.
9. Pour the thawed vegetables around the sides of the meatloaf.
10. When the coals are ready, put the lid on the oven. Place 7 coals under the oven and 14 coals on the lid.
11. Bake the meatloaf for about 1 hour, until the loaf is cooked through. If you pry open the meatloaf a bit with a knife or fork and you see pink meat, keep cooking. You will probably need new coals about 30 to 45 minutes after the lid goes on the oven—so about 45 minutes after starting the first batch of coals, begin a second batch of 21 coals.
12. Once off the coals, pour ¼ cup of barbecue sauce over the meatloaf. Add salt and black pepper to taste.
13. Slice the loaf with a spatula and serve with the vegetables.

Servings: 4–6
Preparation time: 1 hour and 30 minutes

Corn Casserole

½ cup (1 standard stick) butter
2 eggs
1 (15-ounce) can whole-kernel corn
1 (15-ounce) can creamed corn
1 (8.5-ounce) package Jiffy corn
   muffin mix
1 (8-ounce) container sour cream
Cooking spray

EQUIPMENT:

10-inch Dutch oven
Large mixing bowl
Can opener
Long-handled spoon
Fork

PREPARATION:

1. About an hour before starting the coals, set a stick of butter in a warm location to soften.
2. Prepare 21 briquettes for the Dutch oven.
3. Crack the eggs into the bowl, then mix them by stirring very quickly with a fork.
4. Add the can of whole-kernel corn, including its juice, and the can of creamed corn to the bowl with the eggs. Drop the softened stick of butter into the bowl.
5. Pour the contents of the package of corn muffin mix into the bowl along with the sour cream. Stir all of the ingredients together.
6. Spray the inside of the Dutch oven with cooking spray, then pour the ingredients from the bowl into the oven.
7. Place the oven over 7 coals, with 14 on the lid. Bake for 45 minutes to 1 hour or until the top of the casserole becomes golden and a knife or toothpick inserted into the cornbread comes out clean.

Servings: 8-10
Preparation time: 1 hour and 15 minutes

Cornish Game Hens

1 medium-sized onion

3 carrots

2 medium-sized red potatoes

2 (about 1½-pound)
    Cornish game hens

1 (14.5-ounce) can chicken broth

Salt and ground black
    pepper to taste

EQUIPMENT:

10-inch camp Dutch oven

Knife

Can opener

PREPARATION:

1. Prepare 23 briquettes for the Dutch oven.
2. Slice up the onion, peel and cut the carrots into about 1-inch pieces, and cut the potatoes into sort of small pieces.
3. Set the hens in the Dutch oven.
4. Arrange the vegetables around the hens.
5. Pour the chicken broth over the hens and vegetables.
6. Put the lid on the oven. Using 16 coals on the lid and 7 under the oven, bake for about 1 hour, until the skin is golden and a fork can easily pierce the flesh, revealing no remaining trace of pink meat. Refresh the coals as required.
7. Serve with salt and black pepper to taste.

Servings: 4–6
Preparation time: 1 hour and 15 minutes

Cinnamon Bites

2 teaspoons ground cinnamon

1 cup brown sugar

Pillsbury Original Grands!
   refrigerated biscuits

1 cup heavy cream

EQUIPMENT:

10-inch Dutch oven

Small bowl

Heavy-duty aluminum foil

Large wooden spoon

PREPARATION:

1. Prepare 21 briquettes for the Dutch oven.
2. Mix the cinnamon and brown sugar in the small bowl with a spoon.
3. Cover the inside of the Dutch oven with aluminum foil. Press it tightly against the bottom and wall.
4. Open the container of biscuit dough by whomping it on the side of something hard, like a picnic table. Remove the dough and pull it apart into small pieces.
5. Lay the biscuit dough in the Dutch oven.
6. Pour the cream over the biscuits, coating all of them.
7. Sprinkle the biscuits with the cinnamon-sugar mixture.
8. Once the coals are ready, put the lid on the oven. Place 7 coals under the oven and 14 on the lid.
9. Bake the biscuits for about 30 minutes. Allow to cool for a few minutes before serving.

Servings: 8

Preparation time: 45 minutes

Cherry Cobbler

1–2 tablespoons vegetable oil

1 (21-ounce) can cherry pie filling

1 (15.25-ounce) package yellow or white cake mix

¼ cup (½ standard stick) cold butter

¼ cup milk

EQUIPMENT:

10-inch Dutch oven

Heavy-duty aluminum foil

Paper towel

Can opener

PREPARATION:

1. Prepare 21 briquettes for the Dutch oven.
2. Line the Dutch oven with aluminum foil. Using a paper towel and a little vegetable oil, lightly cover the foil with oil.
3. Pour the pie filling over the foil in the Dutch oven.
4. Sprinkle the dry cake mix evenly over the pie filling.
5. Slice the butter into pats and distribute over the cake mix.
6. Pour the milk over all. Do not stir! Place the lid on the oven.
7. Using 14 coals on the lid and 7 under the oven, bake for 40 to 50 minutes, until the cobbler begins to brown.

Servings: 6-8
Preparation time: 1 hour

Foil Cooking

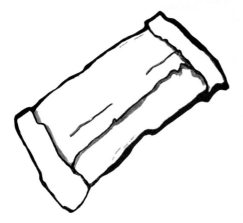

Aluminum foil is aluminum made into thin sheets. Some people call it tin foil, and that's OK, but it really is aluminum. Because the sheets are thin, you can easily bend them and twist them and fold them snugly around just about any shape. Foil does not cost very much. And when you use it, you don't need expensive cooking gear. We're guessing you already know a lot about aluminum foil—but you may not know about all the different recipes it can be used in to cook food outdoors.

The simplest method for cooking with aluminum foil is this: pile some meat and/or veggies and/or fruit on a piece of aluminum foil, wrap it up tightly, and toss it on a grill over your heat source or, sometimes, directly on the coals of a campfire.

As you know by now, we are going to give you more-specific directions in the next few recipes. But remember that, in most cases, the foil needs to be sealed tightly to hold in heat and juices (if there are any). To seal the foil package tightly, where two edges of the foil meet, fold them together once or twice and press to make the seal even tighter. We're guessing foil cooking will become one of your favorite ways to prepare food.

To make foil packets:

1. Start with a heavy-duty sheet of aluminum foil.
2. Cut the sheet to about twice the size of the food being cooked.
3. Place the food in the center of the foil, making sure there is a couple inches or more of room between the food and the edge of the foil.

4. Take two sides of the foil and pull them over the food. Seal the sides by folding them firmly together at the top.

5. Flatten the two remaining sides and fold each of these at the ends. Ensure the folds are secure enough to retain steam and moisture.

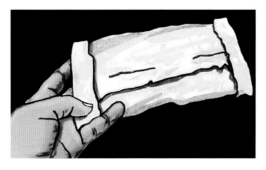

6. Place your foil packet over embers, or on a grill where the food is not in direct contact with the flames. (Foil packets should never be cooked directly over open fire.) Use tongs to flip the packet at least once during the cooking process.

   Tip: To avoid burning your food, a wet newspaper can be placed between two sheets of foil before wrapping. (This will require a second sheet of foil.)

7. Make sure the foil is sealed/folded well so that steam and liquids cannot escape. Steam helps to cook the food not in direct contact with the heat source.

Things about cooking in foil (some bad, some good):

1. Cooking in serving-size packets allows campers to personalize their own meals. Hate onions? Leave them off. Love them? Pile them on!
2. Once your food has cooled, you can eat directly out of the foil packet like you would a plate.
3. Foil cooking reduces cleanup. Imagine a world where there are no pots or plates to clean—that's as close to heaven as we're going to get in the cooking world!

4. Overloading a packet (making it too thick) will keep the heat from fully cooking the inner parts of the packet.
5. You'll need to open the packet occasionally to check how the food hidden in your packet is progressing. Steam and hot liquids will escape when you open your packets, which can lead to burns. Be sure to use tongs and gloves when moving or opening your packets.

Notes: These foil cooking recipes depend on a campfire, which needs to be built in time to let it burn down to hot coals. Do not try to cook over flames.

You may notice that aluminum foil looks shinier on one side. It does not matter which side faces the fire and which side faces the food.

FOIL RECIPES

Breakfast in an Orange

1 large orange
2 eggs
Salt and black pepper to taste

EQUIPMENT:

Heavy-duty aluminum foil
Knife

PREPARATION:

1. Slice the orange in half, then scoop out and eat the contents.
2. Remove any remaining citrus bits, leaving the rind intact.
3. Place each rind "bowl" on a separate large square of foil.
4. Crack an egg into each of the orange bowls.
5. Sprinkle the eggs with salt and black pepper to taste.
6. Wrap foil around each orange rind, being careful not to tilt the bowls.
7. Placed the wrapped oranges upright directly onto the hot embers of a campfire.
8. Cook the oranges for 3 to 5 minutes, depending on the desired firmness of the egg.

Servings: 1
Preparation time: 15 minutes

Campfire Sandwich

1 English muffin or 2
    precooked pancakes
1 fully cooked, round sausage
    patty (can substitute
    precooked bacon)
1 slice cheddar cheese

EQUIPMENT:

Heavy-duty aluminum foil
Long-handled tongs
Knife

JOHNNYGREIG

PREPARATION:

1. Split the English muffin into two rounds, as you would a bagel. If it isn't precut and can't be split by hand, use a knife.
2. Place the sausage patty on the cut side of one of the muffin slices, then set a slice of cheese on top of the sausage.
3. Set the other muffin slice on top, the cut side facing the cheese, to form a sandwich.
4. Tear off a sheet of foil and completely wrap the sausage sandwich in it.
5. Place the wrapped sandwich on a grill grate over the embers in the fire.
6. Cook the sandwich for about 3 to 5 minutes, then flip it with tongs and cook for another 3 to 5 minutes. The sandwich is ready to serve once the cheese is melted.

Servings: 1 (but you can make a lot of these pretty fast)
Preparation time: 15 minutes

Backcountry Bruschetta

Bruschetta, the word and originally the food, comes from Italy. Simply put, it's veggies (and sometimes meat and cheese) served on toasted bread.

2 cups chopped fresh tomatoes
¼ cup chopped fresh basil
1 tablespoon fresh minced garlic
1 tablespoon balsamic vinegar
1 loaf hard-crusted baguette
¼ cup olive oil

EQUIPMENT:

Small mixing bowl
Heavy-duty aluminum foil
Knife

PREPARATION:

1. Combine the tomatoes, basil, vinegar, and garlic in a small bowl.
2. Slice the baguette loaf crosswise into two pieces, then liberally brush the top of each half with olive oil. (You can also cut bread into individual slices.)
3. Wrap each baguette half in a foil pouch and seal the edges tightly.
4. Place the foil pouches on a grate over coals.
5. Bake for about 5 minutes, rotating occasionally, until the bread is toasty.
6. Stir the tomato mixture and spoon over the bread before serving.

LAURIPATTERSON

Servings: 4
Preparation time: 30 minutes

Onion Bombs

4 very large onions
1 pound lean ground beef
½ cup quick-cooking oats
¼ teaspoon garlic powder
Salt, ground black pepper,
   and cayenne pepper to taste
1 tablespoon Worcestershire sauce
1 egg

EQUIPMENT:

Medium-sized mixing bowl
Heavy-duty aluminum foil
Knife

PREPARATION:

1. Cut each onion in half. Remove the outer skin layer as well as the center from each onion, leaving 2 or 3 thick layers that create a half-shell bowl.
2. Dice some of the excess onion pieces to fill ¼ cup.
3. Combine the diced onion, ground beef, oats, seasonings, Worcestershire sauce, and egg in a mixing bowl. Gently knead mixture.
4. Divide the meat mixture among the 8 onion half-shells.
5. Reassemble each onion by aligning the cut layers from 2 halves. Wrap each of the 4 onion balls with a large sheet of foil.
6. Bake directly on hot coals for about 30 minutes, until the meat is thoroughly cooked. If you see pink meat when you open the bombs, put them back in the coals. Occasionally rotate the foil balls while baking.

Servings: 4–8
Preparation time: 45 minutes

Vagabond Packet

1 pound ground beef
1 medium-sized potato, thinly sliced
1 medium-sized onion, thinly sliced
Optional: chopped celery, carrot,
    bell pepper, cabbage
Garlic salt and "Mrs. Dash"
    seasoning blend to taste
4 hamburger buns
Optional toppings: cheese, lettuce,
    tomato slices, ketchup

EQUIPMENT:

Heavy-duty aluminum foil
Knife

PREPARATION:

1. Form 4 hamburger patties from the ground beef. Set each patty on its own piece of foil. The piece of foil must be big enough to completely fold around the patties and the other food.
2. Place the potato and onion slices, along with any optional vegetables, on top of the hamburger patties. Season with garlic salt and Mrs. Dash to taste.
3. Loosely wrap the hamburger and vegetables in the foil while sealing the edges tightly.
4. Place the burger packets on a grate set low over the embers of the campfire and cook for 15 to 30 minutes. Occasionally rotate the packets. The burgers are ready to serve once the pink is gone from the meat.
5. Carefully remove and open the packets, avoiding escaping steam.
6. Place each patty on a hamburger bun with optional cheese and burger toppings. Enjoy the cooked vegetables as a side or on the burger.

Servings: 4
Preparation time: 45 minutes

Mexican Chili Dogs

10 (6-inch) corn or flour tortillas
10 regular-sized hot dogs
1 (15-ounce) can chili with beans
1 (8-ounce) package shredded
    Mexican blend cheese
Optional: chopped lettuce, onion,
    and tomato

EQUIPMENT:

Heavy-duty aluminum foil
Can opener
Long-handled tongs

LAURI PATTERSON

PREPARATION:

1. Cut 10 sheets of aluminum foil, each about 8 to 10 inches long. The size doesn't need to be exact, but the sheets need to be larger than the tortillas. Spread out all the sheets of foil on a clean surface.
2. Place a tortilla in the center of each sheet of foil.
3. Set a hot dog in the center of each tortilla.
4. Top each of the hot dogs with some chili and cheese. Use up all the chili and cheese, and try to divide them evenly on top of all the hot dogs.
5. Roll up each tortilla, then wrap each rolled tortilla in its foil sheet. Be sure that extra foil remains on either end of the tortilla, then twist the foil on the ends so that the tortilla is sealed shut.
6. Use tongs to place the foil packets on a grill grate over the embers in the campfire. Allow the packets to heat for about 10 minutes.
7. Remove the packets from the fire and allow them to cool for a few minutes. Warning: Steam can roll out these foil packets hot enough to burn you!
8. Top with optional ingredients, roll up, and eat.

Servings: 10
Preparation time: 30 minutes

Orange Muffins

4 medium-sized oranges
1 (7-ounce) package Jiffy blueberry
    muffin mix (or something similar)
1 egg
⅓ cup milk

EQUIPMENT:

Knife
Medium-sized mixing bowl
Long-handled spoon
Heavy-duty aluminum foil
Long-handled tongs

PREPARATION:

1. Cut each of the oranges in half.
2. Scoop out the insides of the oranges, being careful not to tear the skins. The insides aren't required for this recipe, so eat up. You'll end up with 8 hollowed-out orange halves, like little bowls.
3. Pour the blueberry muffin mix into the mixing bowl.
4. Crack the egg into the bowl, then add the milk. Stir the ingredients with the spoon until the batter is thick and no large lumps remain.
5. Fill each of the orange halves with muffin batter. Any batter left over can be added to more hollowed-out orange halves, if you have them.
6. Tear off 4 large squares of heavy-duty foil.
7. Align 2 filled orange halves together to form a sphere, working quickly to keep the batter from oozing out. Wrap the sphere tightly in a sheet of foil. Do this for all the orange halves. You should have 4 foil-wrapped filled orange spheres once finished.
8. Set the foil spheres directly onto the hot coals using long-handled tongs.
9. Bake the oranges for about 10 to 15 minutes, at which point the muffin mix should be fully cooked.

Servings: 4
Preparation time: 30 minutes

Cooking on a "Stick"

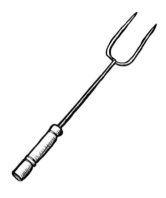

Jabbing a stick into something and holding it over a fire might have been the very first way of cooking. Back then, and for a long time after that, people found their sticks on the ground. And you can still cook that way. Some of the recipes in this section recommend a stick you find on the ground. But today you have choices. You can use a skewer, a long piece of wood or metal with a pointed end. Sometimes metal skewers have wooden handles—and sometimes not. We really like camping forks. A camping fork is, yes, a fork, but a very long fork, usually 2½ to 3 feet long. They keep your hand away from the heat. They don't cost very much. And they are easy to use.

PHOTOALTO/ALE VENTURA

Note: Remember, it's tough to cook anything over a roaring fire. Flames are too hot, so you burn food and maybe your hand. What you need for cooking is hot coals: the coals that are left after the fire roars for a while and then dies down. It takes about an hour for flames to burn down to coals.

Selecting a Stick

- Reduce impact by using only branches collected from the ground and only in areas where downed wood is plentiful and gathering is permitted.
- Your stick should be about as round as a dime and about 3 feet long.
- Never cut green limbs from live trees and shrubs. Use sticks already on the ground. If it's dirty, clean it.

COOKING ON A "STICK" RECIPES

Paper Bag Breakfast

2 thick strips bacon
2 eggs

EQUIPMENT:

Paper lunch bags
Camping fork
Knife

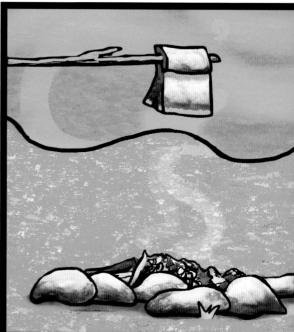

PREPARATION:

1. Cut the bacon strips in half along their length, and lay the pieces side by side in the bottom of a paper lunch bag. If the bag is not sturdy, double up using a bag within a bag.
2. Crack 2 eggs into the bag over the bacon.
3. Roll the top of the bag in flattened sections as you would the end of a tube of toothpaste, and skewer it closed with a camping fork so that the bag hangs at the end of the fork.
4. Toast the food in the bag by holding it with the fork above hot coals, being careful not to set the bag on fire. The rendered bacon fat will be absorbed by the paper and protect the bag from burning. The bag shouldn't drip unless it's torn.
5. Once the eggs become firm, set the bag aside to cool for a few minutes, then carefully tear the bag open to make a bowl. Serve breakfast straight from the bag!

Tip: If the paper trash will be burned in the campfire following breakfast, reduce the risk of wildfire by first tearing the used lunch bag into small pieces or by weighing the bag down once it is in the fire. This will decrease the tendency of the burning ash to float away.

Servings: 1
Preparation time: 15 minutes

Spicy Kabobs

½ cup honey

½ cup lime juice

1 teaspoon ground chipotle pepper

1 teaspoon dried cilantro

1 red bell pepper, cut into wedges

1 sweet onion, cut into wedges

1 pint cherry tomatoes

1 (14-ounce) package smoked
   sausage, cut into 1-inch pieces

EQUIPMENT:

Gallon-sized Ziploc bag

Knife

4 metal skewers

Enjoy kabobs your way!

PREPARATION:

1. Combine the honey, lime juice, chipotle pepper, and cilantro in a gallon-sized Ziploc bag.
2. Add the bell pepper, onion, cherry tomatoes, and smoked sausage to the bag.
3. Seal the bag tightly, shake to coat the vegetables and sausage, then place the bag in a cooler for about 30 minutes to allow the ingredients to marinate.
4. Alternating between vegetables and sausage, thread onto 4 skewers.
5. Set the kabobs on the grill over medium heat. Cook for 10 to 15 minutes, rotating periodically.

Servings: 4

Preparation time: 1 hour

JEREMY WOODHOUSE

Cheese Dogs

1 (16.3-ounce) container Pillsbury Original Homestyle Grands! refrigerated biscuits (or something similar)
8 cheese-filled regular-length hot dogs

Optional: ketchup, mustard

EQUIPMENT:

8 camping forks

PREPARATION:

1. Open the container of biscuit dough and separate the biscuits from each other. There will be 8 of them.
2. Flatten each biscuit into a rectangle about 6 inches long.
3. Place a hot dog in the center of the rectangle and roll the biscuit around it to form a log. Pinch the sides of the dough together to seal it shut. Do this for each hot dog.
4. Spear each dough-covered hot dog with a camping fork.
5. Hold the dough-covered dog over the hot embers, rotating the camping fork often to cook all sides of the dough.

6. Heat the dough until it becomes golden brown all over. Move the hot dog away from the fire, then patiently hold the camping fork for a few minutes while the bread and hot dog cool a little. They can be very hot when you first move them away from the heat!
7. If you want to, put ketchup and/or mustard on the dog before eating.

Servings: 8
Preparation time: 30 minutes

Snakes

1 (16.3-ounce) container Pillsbury Original Homestyle Grands! refrigerated biscuits (or something similar)
1 (8-ounce) can Kraft Sharp Cheddar Easy Cheese
Cooking spray

EQUIPMENT:

8 cooking sticks

PREPARATION:

1. Open the container of biscuit dough and separate the biscuits from each other. There will be a total of 8.
2. Shape each biscuit dough into a "snake" about 1 foot long. Roll out any lumpy parts of the dough so that the snake is evenly thick.
3. Completely cover about 1 foot along the end of each stick with cooking spray, then wrap the dough around the part of the stick covered in oil. Twist the dough around the stick like the stripes on a candy cane, starting at the top end of the stick and working downward. It's OK if the dough touches as you go.

4. Hold the dough-wrapped stick over the hot embers, rotating the stick often to cook all sides of the dough.
5. Heat the dough until it becomes golden brown all over, then remove the stick from over the fire. Patiently hold the stick for a few minutes while the bread cools off.

6. Once the bread cools, carefully wiggle it off the end of the stick.
7. Eat the snake with the Easy Cheese.

Servings: 8
Preparation time: 30 minutes

Chocolate Marshmallows

This is a yummy variation of the famous roasted marshmallow.

Chocolate syrup (you can
   decide how much)
Toppings: shredded coconut,
   Rice Krispies, chopped nuts,
   or sprinkles
1 regular-size marshmallow

EQUIPMENT:

3 small bowls
Camping fork or stick

PREPARATION:

1. In the first bowl put a small amount of water, in the second bowl put the chocolate syrup, and in the third bowl add the topping of your choice.
2. Quickly dip the marshmallow in the bowl of water. The water will help prevent the marshmallow from flaming while over the campfire.
3. Place the marshmallow on a camping fork or stick and toast over the campfire until golden brown.
4. Immediately roll the hot marshmallow in chocolate syrup, followed by a dip in the bowl of topping.

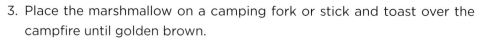

Servings: 1
Preparation time: 15 minutes

Pie Iron Cooking

The first time you see a pie iron, you might not know what you're looking at. Using a pie iron is a unique way to cook over the coals of a fire. It has two metal plates, usually cast iron but sometimes aluminum, that connect by way of a hinge. The two plates may be round or square, and they're hollowed out so there's a space between them when the plates are pressed together—sort of like a clamshell. Both plates have long metal handles.

Here's the fun part: you make a sandwich, put it in the clamshell, close it tightly, and lay it in the coals of a fire. Soon your sandwich is hot, toasted, and sealed around the edges. And you get to choose what kind of sandwich you toast. It can be meat, cheese, veggies, fruit, or any combination. After you read the recipes, you will understand pie irons a lot better.

What's in a Name?

Pie irons have different names in different places. You might hear them called pudgy pie makers, sandwich toasters, toastie makers, and snackwich makers. You might come up with a name you like better!

PIE IRON RECIPES

BUCK TILTON

Encampment Breakfast

2 slices sandwich bread

2 teaspoons butter

1 egg

Salt and ground black
 pepper to taste

Optional: slice of cheese
 (your choice)

EQUIPMENT:

Pie iron

PREPARATION:

1. Butter one side of each slice of bread.
2. Place a slice of bread in one side of the pie iron, butter side against the cast iron.
3. Crack the egg over the center of the bread.
4. Sprinkle the egg with salt and black pepper to taste, then cover with optional cheese.
5. Cover with the second slice of bread, butter side up.
6. Close the pie iron and cook over campfire coals, about 5 minutes per side, until the bread is lightly toasted and the egg cooked through.

Servings: 1

Preparation time: 15 minutes

MILJKO

Note: The long handles and the hinge that holds the plates together allow you to take your pie iron out of the coals and open it up to check on your sandwich. If it needs more time, clamp it back shut and put it back in the coals.

Cinnamon Breakfast Pie

1 (8-ounce) container Pillsbury Original Crescent Rolls (or something similar)
2 tablespoons butter, softened (plus a little more to grease the pie iron)
2 teaspoons ground cinnamon
2 teaspoons brown sugar

EQUIPMENT:

Pie iron
Paper towel

PREPARATION:

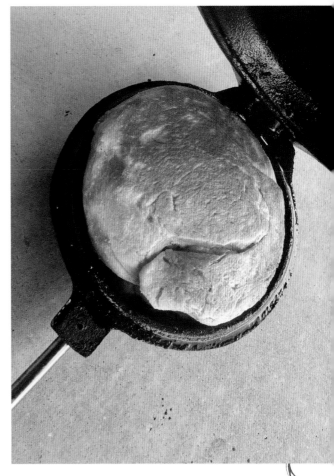

1. Unroll the crescent dough before it warms and becomes sticky.
2. Place a bit of butter on a paper towel and grease the insides of your pie iron.
3. Spread the dough from 2 crescent rolls into each side of the greased pie iron, using the dough from 4 crescents total.
4. Mold the dough to fill and fit both sides of the pie iron.
5. Spread half the butter over each half of the dough.
6. Sprinkle half the cinnamon and brown sugar over each half of the dough.
7. Close the pie iron and cook over hot coals, turning frequently, for about 5 minutes or until the dough becomes golden brown.
8. Allow the iron to cool for a few minutes, then carefully remove the pie from the iron. Repeat steps 2 through 6 for the second pie using the remaining ingredients.

Note: This recipe cooks quickly and burns easily, so pay close attention to cooking time.

Servings: 2
Preparation time: 30 minutes

Pie Iron Pizza

1 tablespoon softened butter
2 slices sandwich bread
1 tablespoon pizza sauce
4 slices pepperoni
1 slice mozzarella cheese
    (or shredded)

EQUIPMENT:

Pie iron

PREPARATION:

1. Spread butter on one side of each slice of bread.
2. Set the bread slices in the pie iron with the buttered sides against the iron surface.
3. Spread the pizza sauce on one slice of bread, then add the pepperoni and cheese.
4. Close the pie iron and cook over the campfire for about 10 minutes, turning occasionally, until the bread is toasted.

Note: If the bread slices are too large for the pie iron, trim to fit before buttering. Or, once the pie iron is clamped shut, you can tear the excess bread off because it will stick out of the pie iron.

Servings: 1
Preparation time: 15 minutes

Pie Iron Delight

Butter or oil to grease the pie iron
2 (¾-inch-thick) slices pound cake
2 tablespoons of your favorite
    pie filling
Whipped cream to taste

EQUIPMENT:

Pie iron
Paper towel

PREPARATION:

1. Place a little butter or oil on a paper towel and grease the insides of the pie iron.
2. Place a slice of pound cake in each side of the greased pie iron.
3. Spread pie filling on one of the slices of cake.
4. Close the pie iron and set over the embers of the campfire.
5. Cook for about 10 minutes, turning occasionally.
6. Serve with whipped cream.

Servings: 1
Preparation time: 15 minutes

Apple Mountain Turnovers

Butter or oil to grease the pie iron
1 tablespoon cream cheese
2 slices sandwich bread
¼ apple, cored, peeled, and sliced into thin wedges
½ teaspoon ground cinnamon
½ teaspoon confectioners' sugar

EQUIPMENT:

Pie iron
Paper towel

PREPARATION:

1. Place a little butter or oil on a paper towel and grease the insides of the pie iron.
2. Spread the cream cheese on one side of a slice of bread and lay on one side of the pie iron, cream cheese side facing up.
3. Lay the apple slices over the top of the cream cheese, then sprinkle the apples with cinnamon and sugar.
4. Cover with the second bread slice.
5. Close the pie iron and hold over the campfire for about 5 to 10 minutes, rotating occasionally, until the apples are soft and hot.

Servings: 1
Preparation time: 15 minutes

How to Set a Simple Picnic Table

Most people treat eating outdoors as a fun, casual experience. Many of the table manners you might be expected to have at home simply don't apply outdoors. Hurray! But there are occasions where you might want your table to look fancier, like a birthday party or when you cook a meal you're proud of. That's why it's always good to know how to set a proper table.

Here are some of the items you'll need:

Large plate for the main meal

Drinking cup

Napkin

2 forks (1 fork is optional)

Knife

Spoon

Optional: smaller plate or bowl for bread or salad

1. Begin by placing the large plate on the table where you plan to eat.
2. Your drinking cup will sit to the upper right of the plate.
3. Fold the napkin horizontally. Lay it to the left of your plate and place either one or two forks on top of the napkin. The reason we sometimes use two forks is because the fork on your far left is your salad fork and the fork closest to your plate is your regular fork. You probably won't need two forks at a picnic, but it's good to know which fork is which in case you are invited to eat with royalty someday.
4. On the right side of the plate, place your knife with its sharp side facing the plate (so it doesn't cut you). Set the spoon down to the right of the knife.
5. If you're planning on having bread or a side salad, you will want to add a smaller plate or bowl to the top left side of the plate.
6. Voila (behold)! That's it!

Mind Your Manners!

Good table manners aren't something we tend to worry about when we're camping, but they can be important in other settings. Do you have good table manners? What do good manners look like exactly? Have you ever been asked to keep your elbows off the table, chew with your mouth closed, or place your knife and fork diagonally across your plate when you're done eating? Those are common customs we find in the US.

Did you know that manners aren't the same throughout the world? Countries and cultures often have their own dining etiquette (table manners), and these might surprise you. Here are some fun examples:

IMAGE SOURCE

- Has anyone ever told you to stop slurping your food? Well, in Japan, slurping your noodles is perfectly OK!
- Do you sometimes wonder whether it's alright to eat a particular food with your hands? In Mexico, it's considered snobby to eat your tacos with a knife and fork!
- What's wrong with asking for a little extra salt or pepper at a meal? We do that all the time in the US. In Portugal and Egypt, this request is considered an offense to the chef, who has already seasoned your food to perfection!
- What kind of reaction would you get if you burped at the table? Burping in China is a compliment to the chef. Burp away!
- What could be more polite than placing your hands on your lap at dinner? In Russia, that would be frowned upon. Instead, your wrists should rest on the edge of the table.
- If you're left-handed, you might want to practice eating with your right hand before your next trip to Africa, the Middle East, or India. Eating with the left hand in these places can be considered unclean.
- Were you taught to finish your meal before leaving the table? The opposite is true in China, where it's customary to leave some food on the plate when you're done. This lets the host know that they've done a good job providing you with more than enough food.
- Saying "thank you" for a nice meal or when someone passes the butter is considered polite in the US. In India, on the other hand, gratitude is unspoken and expressions like "thank you" are reserved for extraordinary acts. In India, helping and serving one another is a cultural expectation and therefore many will find the words "thank you" to be offensive or unnecessary.

Don't forget to brush up on the customs of any country you visit someday!

Cooking Careers

Love cooking and everything food? Good news! There are fun careers and hobbies for foodies like you. Check these out:

- Restaurant chef
- Personal chef
- Food blogger
- Food tester
- Cake decorator
- Food instructor or culinary arts teacher
- Baker
- Caterer
- Food stylist for commercials, TV, magazines, etc.

- Food writer
- Cookbook author
- Restaurant reviewer
- Food photographer
- Recipe developer
- Food scientist
- Food truck owner
- Nutritionist or dietitian
- Restaurant owner

VALENTINRUSSANOV

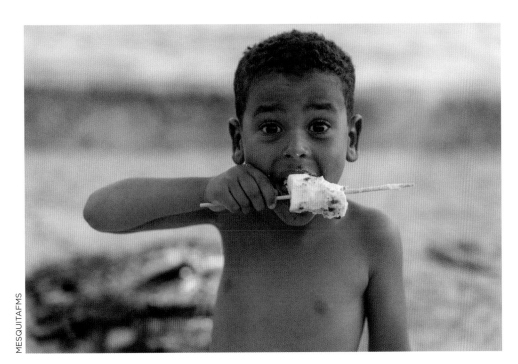
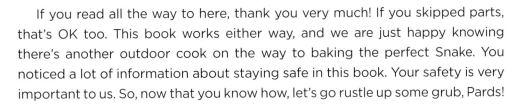

MESQUITAFMS

If you read all the way to here, thank you very much! If you skipped parts, that's OK too. This book works either way, and we are just happy knowing there's another outdoor cook on the way to baking the perfect Snake. You noticed a lot of information about staying safe in this book. Your safety is very important to us. So, now that you know how, let's go rustle up some grub, Pards!

APPENDIX
COMMON MEASUREMENT CONVERSIONS

UNITED STATES VOLUMETRIC CONVERSIONS

1 smidgen	¹⁄₃₂ teaspoon
1 pinch	¹⁄₁₆ teaspoon
1 dash	⅛ teaspoon
3 teaspoons	1 tablespoon
48 teaspoons	1 cup
2 tablespoons	⅛ cup
4 tablespoons	¼ cup
5 tablespoons + 1 teaspoon	⅓ cup
8 tablespoons	½ cup
12 tablespoons	¾ cup
16 tablespoons	1 cup
1 ounce	2 tablespoons
4 ounces	½ cup
8 ounces	1 cup
⅝ cup	½ cup + 2 tablespoons
⅞ cup	¾ cup + 2 tablespoons
2 cups	1 pint
2 pints	1 quart
1 quart	4 cups
4 quarts	1 gallon
1 gallon	128 ounces

Note: Dry and wet volumes are equivalent for teaspoon, tablespoon, and cup.

INTERNATIONAL METRIC SYSTEM CONVERSIONS

VOLUME AND WEIGHT

United States	Metric
¼ teaspoon	1.25 milliliters
½ teaspoon	2.5 milliliters
¾ teaspoon	3.75 milliliters
1 teaspoon	5 milliliters
1 tablespoon	15 milliliters
1 ounce (volume)	30 milliliters
¼ cup	60 milliliters
½ cup	120 milliliters
¾ cup	180 milliliters
1 cup	240 milliliters
1 pint	0.48 liter
1 quart	0.95 liter
1 gallon	3.79 liters
1 ounce (weight)	28 grams
1 pound	0.45 kilogram

TEMPERATURE

°F	°C
175	80
200	95
225	105
250	120
275	135
300	150
325	165
350	175
375	190
400	205
425	220
450	230
475	245
500	260

BRITISH, CANADIAN, AND AUSTRALIAN CONVERSIONS

1 teaspoon (Britain, Canada, Australia)	approx. 1 teaspoon (United States)
1 tablespoon (Britain, Canada)	approx. 1 tablespoon (United States)
1 tablespoon (Australia)	1.35 tablespoons (United States)
1 ounce (Britain, Canada, Australia)	0.96 ounce (United States)
1 gill (Britain)	5 ounces (Britain, Canada, Australia)
1 cup (Britain)	10 ounces (Britain, Canada, Australia)
1 cup (Britain)	9.61 ounces (United States)
1 cup (Britain)	1.2 cups (United States)
1 cup (Canada, Australia)	8.45 ounces (United States)
1 cup (Canada, Australia)	1.06 cups (United States)
1 pint (Britain, Canada, Australia)	20 ounces (Britain, Canada, Australia)
1 imperial gallon (Britain)	1.2 gallons (United States)
1 pound (Britain, Canada, Australia)	1 pound (United States)

Coal-Temperature Conversion Chart

Dutch Oven Diameter		Oven Temperature					
		325°F	350°F	375°F	400°F	425°F	450°F
8"	Total Briquettes	15	16	17	18	19	20
	On Lid	10	11	11	12	13	14
	Underneath Oven	5	5	6	6	6	6
10"	Total Briquettes	19	21	23	25	27	29
	On Lid	13	14	16	17	18	19
	Underneath Oven	6	7	7	8	9	10
12"	Total Briquettes	23	25	27	29	31	33
	On Lid	16	17	18	19	21	22
	Underneath Oven	7	8	9	10	10	11
14"	Total Briquettes	30	32	34	36	38	40
	On Lid	20	21	22	24	25	26
	Underneath Oven	10	11	12	12	13	14
16"	Total Briquettes	37	39	41	43	45	47
	On Lid	25	26	27	28	29	30
	Underneath Oven	12	13	14	15	16	17

RECIPE INDEX

INDEX

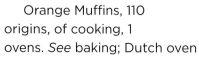

ABOUT THE AUTHORS

Buck Tilton is the author of *Knots for Kids*, *Outdoor Skills for Kids*, *Knack Knots You Need*, *Knack Hiking & Backpacking*, *Knack First Aid*, and *Cooking the One-Burner Way*. Many of his more than 40 books are FalconGuides, including the award-winning *Wilderness First Responder*, and they have sold more than 500,000 copies combined.

Christine Conners is a fine artist who has penned or illustrated more than 16 outdoor books, including *Knots for Kids*, *Outdoor Skills for Kids*, *Lipsmackin' Backpackin'*, and *The Scout's Outdoor Cookbook*. She teaches art and psychology in Tucson, Arizona. Her books can be viewed at www.lipsmackincampin .com and her art at www.artby conners.com.

ACKNOWLEDGMENT

Extra special thanks to Allison Rudick, Girl Scouts of North Central Alabama, for sharing her box and solar oven directions and photos with us!

FALCONGUIDES®

MAKE ADVENTURE YOUR STORY™

Since 1979, FalconGuides has been a trailblazer in defining outdoor exploration. Elevate your journey with contributions by top outdoor experts and enthusiasts as you immerse yourself in a world where adventure knows no bounds.

Our expansive collection spans the world of outdoor pursuits, from hiking and foraging guides to books on environmental preservation and rockhounding. Unleash your potential as we outfit your mind with unparalleled insights on destinations, routes, and the wonders that await your arrival.

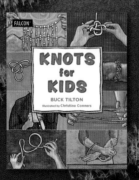
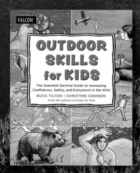

LET FALCON BE YOUR GUIDE